John Conway

Rational Religion

John Conway

Rational Religion

ISBN/EAN: 9783337262426

Printed in Europe, USA, Canada, Australia, Japan

Cover: Foto ©Lupo / pixelio.de

More available books at **www.hansebooks.com**

Rational Religion.

— BY —

REV. JOHN CONWAY,

EDITOR OF "NORTH-WESTERN CHRONICLE," ST. PAUL, MINN.

"*While reason drew the plan, the heart inform'd
The moral page, and fancy lent it grace.*"
THOMSON—*Liberty*, Part IV.

MILWAUKEE:
HOFFMANN BROTHERS,
PRINTERS TO THE HOLY APOSTOLIC SEE.
1890.

PREFATORY NOTE.

THE fact that this book is intended for Catholic readers, is no reason why it should not be useful for non-Catholics. I sincerely hope that our separated brethren, as well as those who are of the household of the Faith, may derive some good from it. I have endeavored to put into what we may call foundation chapters — "The Existence of God," "The Divinity of Christ," "Miracles," etc.—a little more argument and information than are commonly found in popular books on such subjects. My object is not to convince Catholics, but to give them ready reasons for their faith in these subjects now-a-days so much talked of. I will not state as an excuse for defects, that the book has been written during the leisure hours of a busy year. If it is worth reading, then it should be read. If it does not repay perusal, then, no matter under what circumstances it has been written, its place should be with the many furniture books that afflict humanity.

I take this opportunity of thanking the REV. P. R. HEFFRON, D. D., Pastor of the Cathedral, St. Paul, for his many valuable suggestions, and for his kindness in reading my manuscript.

JOHN CONWAY.

THE CATHEDRAL,
    St. Paul,
        Minn.

TABLE OF CONTENTS.

CHAPTER I.
God 9

CHAPTER II.
The Trinity 20

CHAPTER III.
The Divinity of Christ 28

CHAPTER IV.
Miracles 37

CHAPTER V.
Faith and Reason 48

CHAPTER VI.
Faith and Physics 55

CHAPTER VII.
Faith and Evolution 66

CHAPTER VIII.
The Church and the Bible 76

CHAPTER IX.
The Meaning of "Out of the Church no Salvation" 87

CHAPTER X.
Indulgences 97

CHAPTER XI.
Theology of the Devotion to the Sacred Heart. 109

CHAPTER XII.
Veneration of the Blessed Virgin 116

CHAPTER XIII.
The Immaculate Conception 124

CHAPTER XIV.
Mixed Marriages 133

CHAPTER XV.
Divorce 144

CHAPTER XVI.
Is There a Life Beyond the Grave? 154

CHAPTER XVII.
Reading 163

RATIONAL RELIGION.

CHAPTER I.

GOD.

RENAN says, the totality of human experience may be taken as the foundation of a reasonable creed. The sum of this experience tells us that man believes in an Infinite something; that he believes in offering personal devotion to this Infinite something; that the Infinite in some way reveals Itself; that men believe in a self-conscious individuality which survives their bodies; that any violation of the internal sense of right and wrong must, sometime or other, be visited by unhappy consequences. The first revealed name of this Infinite something in the Scripture is Elohim. It is called Jehovah by the Israelites. We say God. The great question with which St. Thomas puzzled his teachers at Monte Cassino is, What is God? Poetic prose-writers may declare God to be a being of infinite beauty and perfection, which human tongue can not express, nor angelic nature comprehend, and yet leave us as much in the dark as ever. As the absence of definition is a frequent cause of misunderstanding, we give one which, for our present inquiry, all educated people, whether believers or unbelievers, will accept.

By God we mean a spirit infinitely perfect, the Creator of heaven and earth, and all things. The existence of God is a preamble of faith. It is also an article of faith, for in the Apostles' and in the Nicene Creed we say, "I believe in God." The Vatican Council teaches that we can get a sure knowledge of God by the natural light of reason and from the consideration of created things. Reason must not be undervalued, for, after all, it is the only faculty we possess to judge of anything, even of revelation. God is not comprehended, nor is He comprehensible; but God is knowable and known. Everything that is knowable is not comprehensible. We comprehend that which the mind fully grasps; for example, that two and two make four, that parallel lines never meet, that contradictories can not be at the same time true. We know of the existence of matter; its essence we can not comprehend. We may analyze water and reduce it to its component parts of oxygen, hydrogen, carbon, and nitrogen; as to its essence, we are just as much as ever in the dark. We can not account for the globular form of the trembling raindrop which the passing storm has suspended from the eaves of our houses; we know that the sun and earth and millions of other planets are suspended in a most subtle medium: what holds them there we may call by scientific names, but we may as well candidly admit that it is a mystery as profound as the resurrection of Lazarus. The fact is, incomprehensibility is not a motive for rejecting belief, either in the natural or in the supernatural. With the requisite machinery, the earth can be compressed into the size of a cannon-ball, the ocean can be emptied, the steamship "Alaska" can be floated on a glass of water, but a full idea of God can not be put into the human mind; for the limited can not grasp the infinite. All who do not recognize the existence of God may be classed under the general head of Atheists. Besides those—if such there are—who never heard or thought of a Supreme Being, and those who, having heard of Him, yet refuse to believe in His existence, there are many others who live as though there were no God, grievously setting His laws at defiance—Theists in theory, Atheists in practice. The modern fashionable form of Atheism is called among English-speaking peoples Agnosticism. There may be, or there may not be, a God, the professors of this form of unbelief tell us, but, they continue, we have no proof that there is. An Agnostic is literally a know-nothing, and it is a strange irony of history that whilst modern unbelievers are called Agnostics, the great opponents of faith in the latter part of the second and the whole of the third century were called Gnostics.

The two great causes of Atheism are intellectual abuse and mental depravity. The existence of God can not be proved by algebraical formulas, and some are so intellectually cramped that they can not appreciate any other kind of argument. Bacon truly says that tiny sips of philosophy lead to Atheism, but its more generous draughts bring back to religion. The wish is father to the thought. Some men dislike the duties, the sacrifices and the restraints imposed by God, hence they fain would reason Him out of existence. As the wish not to believe helps largely to infidelity, so the wish to believe is a great aid to faith. To the Christian, God is not the "Unknowable" of Herbert Spencer, nor the "Universum" of Strauss, nor the "Humanity" of Comte and Harrison, nor the "Immensities" of Carlyle, but He is a Being of surpassing beauty and loveliness, of bounteous charity and even-handed justice.

Scientists are fond of invading the domain of theology, and doing the unscientific thing of applying the principles of physical science to the problems of sacred knowledge. Let us take them on their own ground for a moment. If there be any one thing about which scientists agree, it is the existence of motion. We know matter by its properties, and motion is not an essential property of matter. If it were, then all matter, and every particle of it, would be continuously in motion. Motion exists. The thing moved must have a mover. Whence that motion? Not from itself, for nothing can be, under the same aspect, at once the cause and the subject of motion. Even intelligent beings can not be the independent cause of their own movements. The mind can not think unless some object has been presented to it. So that it comes to this, we have to fall back on God as the first mover of the universe. Indeed, the very misery which Agnostics or know-nothings have to endure, is in itself an argument in favor of Theism; as witness the Hogarthian series of maddening pictures of woe unutterable so frequently before the mind of that representative of his class,—Langham, of "Robert Elsmere." The Christian dogma, "I believe in God the Father Almighty," is more reasonable than the rationalistic dogma, "I believe in Nature the Mother Almighty." The very origin of life can not be explained without God. Life is a spontaneous, or internal and uninterrupted movement. It is spontaneous, for it comes from an internal principle of action. It is uninterrupted, because, in all organic things, it goes on from its beginning till what we call death. It may spring from matter containing a vital principle; it can not spring from dead matter, for dead matter, like the mineral world for example, having no principle of life, can not spring into action. With the shadow of death immediately succeeding the glow of life, its universal reign, and the inherent perishableness of all things before us, the mind can look through the dim past, to a time when there was no song of a wild bird, and no rustle of a leaf, and no fragrance of a flower, and looking out on that dreary waste of a dead world, it easily draws the conclusion: life must be from a self-existing and necessary Being—God. Something exists. The idealist Berkeley, who said things exist only because we think they exist, has few followers nowadays; and if anyone still doubts real existence, he has only to wait a few hours till he grows hungry or thirsty, or let him go out in a snow-storm, and his idealism will soon vanish before the stern reality of things. Whatever exists, then, is either necessary and eternal, or is dependent and created. If the former, it is God; if the latter, it leads up to God. I say it leads up to God, because the dependent and created is neither possible nor intelligible without the eternal. We can not conceive a thing to be and not to be at the same time; we can not form an idea of a square circle or of a thinking stone; equally impossible is it for the mind to conjure up an idea of a thing which is perishable and self-subsisting. To deny the existence of God is to be guilty of self-contradiction. To assert the creation of things from nothing, without a Being of Infinite Power, is to say what is unthinkable. To tell me that things are produced in an infinite series, makes me ask, Whence comes the first link in the chain of the series? To tell me that the world accounts for its own existence without a Supreme Being, is as intelligible as to say that Brooklyn Bridge accounts for its own existence without a builder. Take anything you please, it is the effect of some cause, and this latter of some other cause, and so on until we come to the First Cause—God. Cardinal Newman sums up the argument in these words : " For if (to suppose what is absurd) the maker of the visible world was himself made by some other maker, and that maker again by another, you must anyhow come at last to a first Maker, who had no other, that is, who had no beginning. Else you will be forced to say that the world was not made at all, or made itself, and itself had no beginning, which is more wonderful still ; for it is much easier to conceive that a spirit, such as God is, existed from eternity, than that this material world was eternal. Unless, then, we are to doubt that we live in a world of beings at all, unless we doubt our own existence, if we do but grant that there is something or other now existing, it follows at once that there must be something which has always existed, and never had a beginning." Suppose we go back to a time when the "first womb of things was pregnant with all the future," even then we must ask ourselves, Is the plant from the seed, or the seed from the plant? the hen from the egg, or the egg from the hen? Neither the first seed nor the first egg produced itself.

Order is unity in variety. The universal prevalence of order shows the world to have been framed by a Being of the highest knowledge and power. There are evidences of design on all sides. Its marks are unmistakable. The laws which govern the physical world must come from intelligence. As a recent writer points out, rudely-cut stone hatchets, or flint arrow-heads, or Swiss lake-dwellings, or mounds of marine shells on the shores of Denmark, are considered to be tokens of intelligent action, or of the existence of pre-historic man. The same line of reasoning, applied to the physical world, leads up to the highest intelligence —to God Himself. Tell me not that science has disposed of religion. It is one thing to know of the existence of the Author of religion; it is another to be able to tell the *how* of His existence. Suppose we found a steam-engine, or a watch, or any other piece of mechanism, in the heart of the Dark Continent, or in dead cold grasp of an ice-bound valley of Greenland, or in an island of the Indian Ocean where we have no record that human foot ever left its print upon the sandy beach or human voice ever broke the stillness of the air, is not the presence of one or other of these things undeniable proof that an intelligent being had reached these places? The universe is a much more complicated piece of machinery than any that man can make. The sun is three hundred thousand times as heavy as the earth, yet the whole solar system is a very small part of the vast universe—a drop in the infinite ocean of space. We travel with the earth around the sun at a rate greater than one thousand miles per minute, and other planets travel much faster. Notwithstanding the vastness of the universe, and the marvelous speed of its parts, yet its motion never stops and its machinery is never out of gear. No wonder Voltaire should have said :

"The more I think, the greater my surprise,
No maker formed the clock that moves before my eyes."

It is told of a gambler that, one day, when throwing dice he threw the highest possible number. A bystander said, it is possible to do so once by chance. But the dice-thrower turned up the highest number a second, and a third, and a fourth time. The on-lookers all declared that the dice were loaded. When we look at the wonderful order of the universe, and think of its regularly recurring cycles of almost limitless details, ever keeping their places in spite of many chances of disturbance, and even destruction, we, too, may say nature is loaded. It is loaded, for there is a God behind it. The glorious sun which gives us rosy-fingered morn, time repeating its perpetual poem of the year, violets spreading their velvet blossoms to the day, spendthrift roses giving their perfume to the air, seasons coming and going, rain falling in pleasant showers, light hanging its seven-hued banners on cataract and cloud, spring with deft and unseen fingers weaving the tapestries of green, autumn reaping the wealth of leaf and seed, winter etching in frost the pines and firs, wind and wave changing and destroying, the starry heavens looking down serenely upon us, all tell us of design and point to an intelligent maker and preserver. No wonder St. Paul taught that those who refuse to believe in God are inexcusable. "His invisible things from the creation of the world, are clearly seen, being understood by the things that are made. His eternal power also and divinity; so that they (*i. e.*, the brethren who did not believe in the true God) are inexcusable" (Rom. i. 20).

Society and conscience, as well as nature and intelligence, proclaim a Supreme Being. The great leaders of intellectual hosts in every age have been believers in the Christian religion, and therefore in God. There is in every one an inextinguishable craving after God. Belief in Him is deeply rooted in man's nature. The conclusion that God exists is in man's nature, and all the reasoning in the world will not drive it out. Go to any land you please, to the people cursed with Boötian dullness, or blessed with the highest mental development; to the philosophical Teuton, or the theological Spaniard; to the fair Caucasian, or the dark Ethiopian; to the cold mountains of arctic clime, or to the sweltering valley of equatorial temperature; to the rudest Indian nation, or to the highest product of white civilization,—everywhere you will find a belief in a Supreme Being, perhaps a hazy belief, mingled with superstitions, perverted even to demon-worship, but yet a belief in a Supreme One. In ancient Greece he was Zeus; in Rome, Jupiter; in India, Brahma; in Phœnicia, Baal; in America, amongst our aborigines, the Great Spirit. Every race has a religion of some kind, so that Professor Tiele calls it "an universal phenomenon of humanity."

We reason from conscience up to God. It is the connecting link between the creature and his Creator. Certain things call forth in us approval or blame, and consequently we say they are right or wrong. Conscience may become dull, but it can not be completely stifled. As a sanction of what we call right, and as a reproof of what we call wrong, it furnishes materials for the apprehension of a Divine Judge. If a man commit some immorality, even though it be no offense against society, even though there be no visible eyes upon him, yet he feels a certain confusion and sense of guilt. Conscience is even more than a moral sense: it implies the existence of a living object towards which it is directed. The image of a lifeless thing in the mind does not arouse the affection nor excite any responsibility. The fact that we feel this responsibility is evident that there is One to Whom we are responsible. As we have remorse after having wounded the feelings of a very dear friend, or possess a sunny serenity of mind at having secured the approbation of one whose opinion we highly prize, so there must be within us an image of one in whose smile we find pleasure, in whose frown, pain. The law engraved on our hearts, though it may be blurred over by false teachings and the sway of passion, unceasingly proclaims its force and will not be silenced by any pressure. Why is it there is no rest for the wicked? Why does he flee when no one pursues him? It is because, even though his sin be unknown to his fellow-men, yet his terrified conscience gives him a picture of a Supreme Judge—God.

History also furnishes its share of evidence to the existence of a Supreme Being. No critic of any note nowadays questions the authenticity of the Gospel narratives. We have contemporary records of Christ and His works, written either by eye-witnesses, or by those who were in immediate communication with them. These records, now admitted by all criticism worthy of the name, tell us of the Lord's Prayer, of the Sermon on the Mount, of the Passion, all of which point out Christ's belief in the Fatherhood of God, so that, if Jesus Christ preached that sermon, made those promises, and taught that prayer, then any one who says we know nothing of God, or of a future life, or of an unseen world, says that he does not believe Jesus Christ. With the cumulative evidence of the voice of history, and the voice of conscience, and the voice of all peoples, and the clear signs of intelligent design in the universe, and the existence and creation of all things, after all, God is not quite so unknowable as Herbert Spencer would have us believe. The invitation of the Chief Magistrate of the United States, asking Christians of all denominations to give thanks on the centennial day of civil government of America, not to a myth, but to a God, is a national manifestation of the belief of our people, and of their submission to the will of the God of nations, in spite of the shallow sneers of an Ingersoll.

CHAPTER II.

THE TRINITY.

CATHOLIC doctrine teaches us that in one God there are three persons: the Father, the Son and the Holy Ghost, equal yet distinct, each all-powerful because divine, and all having one and the same divine essence. Three and one, said St. Augustine; three in person, one in essence, is what God is, according to the teaching of the Catholic Church. We believe in a personal God. It is the belief of Catholics that this essential feature of God's nature repeats itself in three distinct ways, so that instead of one Personality in God there are three distinct Persons, and He is Father, Son, or Holy Spirit, according as we view Him in one or other Personality. By reason of the Divine Infinitude that One Personal Being is really Three, whilst He is absolutely One. On the Trinity depend the Incarnation, Death, and Resurrection of Christ; on it depends the equality of the Three Divine Persons who constitute the Godhead; on it depends the oneness of essence in God. Reject it and you set aside the satisfaction made by a Divine Christ for mankind; you eschew the whole system of doctrines which grows out of the Redemption. There are mysteries in nature, and we must not be surprised to find some in revelation. Even the mysterious presents some things which can be understood. The Trinity may be resolved into a number of truths, any one of which is easily intelligible. God is one. The Father is God. The Son is God. The Holy Ghost is God. The Father is not the Son. The Son is not the Holy Ghost. The Holy Ghost is not the Father.

Thus far there is no mystery. Each truth contained in any of the foregoing propositions may well be apprehended. Each may be the object of real assent. Even the very words used—Father, Son, Holy Spirit, God, Three, One,—are in a sense clear and popular, and calculated to call up images in the mind. Religion deals with realities and particulars. It may well flourish on the truths proposed, and in them find motives for devotion and affection. The mystery consists in reconciling these different truths. How are these seven statements at the same time true? How is God One, and yet Three in Person; so that the Father is all that we mean by the word God, and the Son is all that we mean by the word God, and the Holy Ghost is all that we mean by the word God? Does not the idea of one exclude the idea of three, and *vice versa?* Herein consists the mystery. The brightest human intellect can not grasp it. "In the Beatific vision of God," says a well-known modern writer, "shall we, through His grace, be found worthy of it, we shall comprehend clearly what we now dutifully repeat and desire to know, how the Father Almighty is truly and by Himself God, the Eternal Son truly and by Himself God, and the Holy Ghost truly and by Himself God, and yet not Three Gods but One God." We must not conclude that therefore the Trinity ought to be rejected. It would be a very poor process of reasoning to say, because we do not understand the *how* of a thing, it does not, on that account, exist. On the same principle we should refuse to believe in the mysteries of nature, although we know of their existence. The Trinity itself is a mystery; its existence is not mysterious. It is concealed from us under one aspect; it is made known to us under another. It is hidden from us in the sense that we can not see how all the statements of which the doctrine is composed can, when taken together, be true. We know there is within us an invisible, living, thinking faculty which we call soul; that it is united to the body and to every part of the body. How it is united, how it works in the body, why it continues united to the body for a certain length of time, why it does not fly from the body at any moment and leave it a soulless, sightless thing, are questions we can not answer. Yet experience, which is only a partial standard of our judgment, tells us that the soul is united to the body in the manner indicated. Thus does experience outstrip reason. Why, then, we may well ask, should reason be a fetter on our belief in matters entirely outside its province? No wonder St. Paul should have written: "O, the depth of the riches, of the wisdom and of knowledge of God! How incomprehensible are his judgments, and how unsearchable his ways" (Rom. xi. 33). We can not prove the existence of the Trinity from reason. There is not on that account any opposition between them. It is above, not contrary, to reason. There is no contradiction in the doctrinal statement that God is one in *essence* and three in person. A faint illustration may be drawn from the human soul. It is one, yet it has three distinct powers: the memory, the understanding, and the will. Man is one, yet he is threefold in life—animal, rational, and vegetative.

The Trinity, though a mystery, and therefore concealed from us under one aspect (otherwise it would be no mystery), is made known to us under another. Though outside the domain of reason a knowledge of it comes to us from the second great source of truth—revelation. Saints of the Old Testament seem to have had a knowledge of the Trinity. That grand old book points out many parts of the Trinitarian doctrine. The Unity of God was certainly an article of Israel's faith. In Genesis we read : "And God said let us make man to our image and likeness " (i. 26). The words, "God said," prove the Unity of the Godhead; the words, " Let us make man," point to a plurality of persons in the Godhead. Many other passages of the Old Testament indicate that there are more persons than one in God ; for example : "The Lord said to my Lord, sit thou on my right hand" (Psalm cix. 1); "The Lord said to me : you are my Son, I have begotten you to-day " (Psalm ii. 7).

The two chief writers of the New Testament, John and Paul, are full of references to fragments of the doctrine of the Trinity, to truths that are meaningless unless we accept the Trinity. They tell us of the love of the First Person, the grace of the Second, the influence of the Third; they tell us of the foreknowledge of the Father, the Blood of Jesus Christ, the sanctification of the Spirit ; they tell us we are to " pray to the Holy Ghost, abide in the love of God, and look for the mercy of Jesus ; " they are forever ringing the changes on the various truths into which the Trinity may be resolved.

Let us take a step further and yet not in the dark. We find the doctrine of the Trinity distinctly stated in the New Testament. The absolute unity of God is emphatically stated throughout. "To God, the only wise, through Jesus Christ, to whom be honor and glory forever and ever" (Rom. 16, 27). "And this is life everlasting; that they may know the only true God, * * *" (John xvii. 3). "Which in his times he shall show, who is the Blessed and only Mighty, the King of kings and Lord of lords" (I Tim. vi. 15). The New Testament also teaches that there are Three Persons really distinct and divine in God. This, taken in connection with the Unity of God, is the doctrine of the Blessed Trinity. All who believe in the existence of a Supreme Being admit the divinity of God the Father. If any of the Three Persons be God, it is the Father, for He is the source of the other Two. The three Creeds, the Apostles', the Nicene, and the Athanasian, profess a belief in God the Father Almighty. The distinct existence and divinity of the Son is taught with singular lucidity and noteworthy iteration in the Gospel of St. John: "In the beginning was the Word, and the Word was with God, and the Word was God. The same was in the beginning with God. All things were made by Him and without Him was made nothing that was made" (i. 1–3). The Word was the Second Person of the Blessed Trinity, or Jesus Christ; for, later on in this chapter of St. John's Gospel, we are told that this same Word became flesh and dwelt amongst us. The Word was in the beginning, that is, from all eternity, and therefore God. All things were made by this Word. Hence, again, we conclude that the Word is God, for none but God can create. That the personality of the Second Person is a distinct one, is clear from the phrase, "And the Word was with God," that is, in active communication with God the Father. As the spoken word is distinct from the speaker, so is the Divine Word distinct from God the Father. The New Testament also tells us of the divine and distinct personality of the Holy Ghost. The stern, hard words of Peter, when reproaching Ananias, state that the Holy Ghost is God. "Why hath Satan tempted thy heart, that thou shouldst lie to the Holy Ghost? * * * * * Thou hast not lied to man, but to God" (Acts v. 3, 4). His distinct personality is asserted in the words of St. Paul: "All these things one and the same Spirit worketh, dividing to each separately, as He wills" (I Cor. xii. 11).

The doctrine of the Trinity is also revealed to us in these words: "Go ye therefore and teach all nations, baptizing them in the name of the Father, and of the Son, and of the Holy Ghost" (Math. xxviii. 19). Here the Three Persons are mentioned as really distinct. Baptism is administered in the name of the Son and in the name of the Holy Ghost, as well as in the name of the Father. Lest we should load down the page with texts we shall merely give one more, and this time from the Apostle of love, St. John. His words are: "But when the Paraclete shall come which I will send to you from the Father, the Spirit of truth, who proceedeth from the Father, He shall give testimony of Me" (xv. 26). It is Christ who uses these words. He speaks of Himself; He speaks of the Paraclete or Holy Spirit; He speaks of the Father; He points out the Trinity of Persons in the one Godhead.

There is in the Church a very old practice of making the sign of the Cross, saying at the same time: "In the name of the Father, and of the Son, and of the Holy

Ghost, Amen." It is a profession of faith in the Blessed Trinity, and Tertullian, an able writer of the second century, tells us what was the belief of the Church in his time on this matter. He writes: "In all our actions, when we come in or go out, when we dress, when we walk, at our meals, before retiring to sleep, * * * * we form on our foreheads the sign of the Cross. These practices are not recorded by a formal law of Scripture, but tradition teaches them, custom confirms them, faith observes them."

The old and universal belief of the Church in the doctrine of the Blessed Trinity is expressed in the words: Glory be to the Father, and to the Son, and to the Holy Ghost.

The Athanasian Creed has been well called the war-song of faith. Whether this symbol was drawn up by St. Athanasius or not, certain it is, that it is a very full statement of our doctrine of the Trinity, and that it was universally received at a very early period in the history of the Church. Though Adam and his wife may smile at the claims of long descent, yet it is consoling to know when there is question of some point of doctrine, that it is the same now as that which was taught at a time when all say the Catholic Church was the only true Church on earth. The Athanasian Creed says: "This is Catholic faith, that we worship one God in the Trinity, and the Trinity in Unity, neither confounding the Persons nor separating the substance. The Person of the Father is distinct from that of the Son and of the Holy Ghost; the Person of the Son is distinct from that of the Father and of the Holy Ghost; the Person of the Holy Ghost is distinct from that of the Father and of the Son. But of the Father and of the Son and of the Holy Ghost there is one divinity, equal glory, co-eternal majesty. As is the Father, such is the Son, such is the Holy Ghost." Then the Creed tells us of the immensity, the eternity and the omnipotence of each Person: that each Person is God, and yet not three Gods but one; that each Person is Lord, and yet not three Lords but one. The relationship which exists between the Three Persons of the Adorable Trinity is next pointed out. Though the Three Persons existed from all eternity—for each is truly God—yet the Son proceeds from the Father by generation, and the Holy Ghost comes from the Father and the Son by procession. The Father looks into His own essence as into a limitless ocean or boundless mirror, and there sees His own image or exemplar, and that image is the Son. The Father loves the Son with an infinite and eternal love; the Son returns the affection; and that mutual love is the Holy Spirit. That the Son and the Holy Spirit come from the Father is no reason why they should not be eternal as is the Father. Light is the product of the great day-star. It is the principle of light, and yet light is as old as the sun. The moment the latter began to be, it could not help shining and its lustre immediately gave light and heat. Similarly from all eternity the Father saw His image, or God the Son, and from all eternity the Father and the Son loved each other, and this love, or God the Holy Ghost, was from all eternity. We accept revelation. We find the doctrine of the Trinity contained in it. If there were a contradiction in the doctrine Jesus Christ would have known it.

CHAPTER III.

THE DIVINITY OF CHRIST.

WE should try to know as well as to believe; to understand, while we pray. If Christ be not divine, Christianity is a mere human institution, a mere system of natural religion, and worthy of no more respect than any other well-developed and systematized form of philosophy. If Christ be God, then the religion which He tells us it was His mission to establish must also be divine.

All the ancient people looked forward to a Messiah. It is somewhat remarkable to find the inhabitants of ancient Greece and Rome, and India and Egypt, and the aborigines of America, and indeed all the nations of antiquity, unanimous in holding the doctrines of man's fall; the necessity of propitiatory sacrifice; and the redemption of man by a divine Redeemer; so that it would seem these doctrines belonged to a primitive revelation made to our first parents. Besides the belief in these truths, preserved in the midst of so much error and corruption, the dispersion of the chosen people prepared the nations of the earth for the coming of the Messiah. In the words of Genesis, "I will put enmity between thee and the woman, and thy seed and her seed," etc. (iii. 15), we find a promise of the Messiah. A promise was made to Abraham that in him all the nations of the earth should be blessed; Jacob foretold that the sceptre should not pass from Juda till the coming of Him who was the Expected of nations, and He was to establish, not a national religion, but an universal one. The sceptre had passed from the house of Juda; Daniel's seventy weeks of years had been completed; the second temple had been still standing, before the Messiah appeared. We may well ask ourselves where would the world be to-day if that Galilean Peasant had not been born, and lived, and loved, and died for us? The fulfillment of the prophecies in Jesus Christ shows Him to have been the promised Messiah. It was foretold that the Jews should be dispersed by way of punishment for not having received Christ; after His death they were scattered, and ever since have been wanderers on the face of the earth. The public life of the Saviour was to have been a life of many miracles; the Gospels—those brief sketches of His career—show how He quelled the tempest, healed the sick, raised the dead to life, etc. He was to have been born at Bethlehem; that obscure village has been made forever famous by His birth. He was to have come from the family of David; Mary, His mother, belonged to that royal house. He was to have died for our sins; the Evangelists write with such a fullness of detail and such an independence of narration as to put the actuality of His death beyond all reasonable doubt.

Christ is more than a mere messenger from God, such as were the prophets. It has become fashionable to speak of Him as a Plato, a Socrates, an Aristotle, a Pythagoras, a Zoroaster, a Confucius, a Mohammed, or as some great man who, they say, has been raised up for a special purpose. Even if Christ were a great philosopher and nothing more, or a great philanthropist and only that, yet people should love Him much as they reverence any great benefactor of the human race. It is not enough to say that God dwells in Him, as He does in every just man; nor will it do to say that the divinity is in Him preëminently. We hold and teach that Christ is as truly and properly God as the Father and the Holy Spirit. The true doctrine of the divinity of Christ is, that He is one in person, that He has two natures, the human and the divine—the human received from Mary, quickened by the Holy Spirit; the divine coming from the Father from all eternity. The human nature is perfect. The human body of Christ is a perfect human body; the human soul of Christ is a perfect human soul. Christ's human soul possesses self-consciousness, not, however, having final dominion over itself, for it meets divine consciousness and knows that it belongs to a divine person, to whom all its acts are referred. Christ is omnipotent, eternal, infinite; these attributes He has from His divine nature. We say He suffered and died; these are compatible only with human nature. Christ is the embodiment of Christianity, and therefore the target for all its opponents. In the early days of Christianity the attack was led by Celsus, and was of a low, vulgar, filthy kind. The attacks of the last century were remarkable for their coarseness, their slanders, their denunciations. The modern style is gentler and comparatively appreciative. They speak of Christ in language of dulcet tenderness; they speak of Him as having brought calmness, and beauty, and gentleness among men; they speak of Him as being greater than any of the philosophers, and as having established a moral code superior to anything hitherto known in the world. This is not enough for us. We want a divine Christ, divine with the divinity of God the Father, or God the Holy Ghost.

The divinity of Christ is an article of Catholic faith. In that very old summary of doctrine, the Apostles' Creed, we profess our belief in Jesus Christ, the only Son of God, who was conceived by the Holy Ghost and born of the Virgin Mary, suffered under Pilate, was crucified, dead and buried, and rose again from the dead the third day. In the Nicene Creed we say: "And in one Lord Jesus Christ, the only-begotten Son of God, and born of the Father before all ages, God of God, light of light, true God of true God, begotten not made, consubstantial to the Father by whom all things were made." In the Athanasian Creed, Christ is called perfect God and perfect Man.

The texts of the Old and of the New Testament, asserting in various ways the divinity of Christ, are almost innumerable. In the New Testament He is constantly and everywhere called *The* Son of God. He is called the Son of God by the Father: "And He was there until the death of Herod, that it might be fulfilled which the Lord spoke by the prophet saying, out of Egypt have I called my Son" (Math. ii. 15). He calls Himself the Son of God: "All things are delivered to me by my Father, and no one knoweth the Son but the Father, neither doth any one know the Father but the Son, and he to whom the Son will reveal Him" (Math. xi. 27). He is called the Son of God by the angel Gabriel: "He shall be great and shall be called the Son of the Most High, and the Son of God shall give unto him the throne of David his father, and he shall reign in the house of Jacob forever"

(Luke i. 32). He is called the Son of God by the inspired writers, by the disciples and others of the faithful: "Then they that were in the ship came and worshiped Him, saying, Thou art truly the son of God" (Math. xiv. 33). The circumstances in which the title, *The* Son of God, is applied to Him, are noteworthy. In the New Testament we find the phrase, *sons of God*, a common name applied to all men who enjoy His friendship; in the Old Testament the name *a son of God* is used on one or two occasions, but never as a proper name, never as a peculiar and distinguishing title, such as is the title, *The* Son of God, given to Christ. When we speak of the Virgin, all Catholics know we refer to Mary, the mother of God. When we speak of the proto-martyr everybody knows we mean St. Stephen. When we mention the Prince of the Apostles it is well known that St. Peter is the one to whom we refer. In like manner is the name, *The* Son of God, Christ's distinguishing title. This proper name is a proof of His divinity. Let us take an example: The Jews accused Him of breaking the Sabbath because He cured the lame man on the Lord's day. Christ's answer was: "My Father worked until now, and I work" (John v. 17). The Jews understood Him by this expression to claim that He was God. "Hereupon, therefore, the Jews sought the more to kill Him, because He did not only break the Sabbath, but also said that God was His Father, making himself equal to God" (John v. 18). They rightly understood Him. If they did not, He would have been bound as an honest man—and nobody ever impeached Christ's honesty—to correct their error. What does He do? So far from rejecting the interpretation put upon His language, He reasserts, in the clearest words, His divinity: "Amen, amen I say unto you, the Son cannot do anything of Himself, but what the Father doeth, for what things soever He doeth, these the Son also doeth in like manner" (v. 19). He even goes on to confirm His statement of His own divinity by evidence drawn from various sources. He confirms it by the authority of John the Baptist: "There is another that beareth witness of me, and I know that the witness which he witnesseth of me is true. You sent to John and he gave testimony of the truth" (v. 32, 33). He appeals to the evidence of His own works: "But I have a greater testimony than that of John. For the works which the Father hath given me to perfect, the works themselves which I do, give testimony of me, that the Father hath sent me" (36). He appeals to the testimony of His Father: "And the Father Himself, who hath sent me, hath given testimony of me" (37). Finally He appeals to the testimony of Holy Scriptures: "Search the Scriptures, for you think in them to have life everlasting, and the same are they that give testimony of me" (39).

St. John's purpose in writing his Gospel was to teach us that Jesus is the Son of God; and that believing, we may have life in His name. The very first chapter of that Gospel abounds with proofs of Christ's divinity. We read: "In the beginning was the Word, and the Word was with God, and the Word was God. All things were made by Him, and without Him was made nothing that was made. * * * And the Word was made flesh, and dwelt among us." * * * (John i. 15).

The Second Person of the Trinity proceeds from the Father, as a word from the mouth, or as wisdom from the mind. He is called the Word. The phrase, "Word of God," has had its place in the philosophic language of Greece since the days of Plato. We reason in this way : Christ is the Word. The Word is God. Therefore Christ is God. That Christ is the Word is evident. St. John says that the Word was the light of men, that John the Baptist gave testimony of the light, that the " Word was made flesh and dwelt among us."

That the Word is God there is marvelous proof in this Gospel. The Word was in the beginning; that is, before time was, and therefore from all eternity, and therefore is God. This reasoning is strengthened by the following words from the seventeenth chapter : "And now glorify thou me, O Father, with thyself, with the glory I had before the world was, with thee " (5). But the divinity of Christ is stated with striking directness in the last clause of the first verse of the Gospel of St. John : "And the Word was God." Creation is the production of a thing from nothing. The immeasurable abyss which separates nothingness from existence requires divinity to overcome it. This obstacle vanishes in the presence of the Divine Word, for we are told that all things were made by Him (2). The Word, then, is the Creator, hence is God ; and, as the Word is Christ, we lawfully conclude : therefore Christ is God.

Divine honors were paid to Christ. Adoration such as is due to God was given Him. He allowed the man born blind, the pious women, and His disciples to pay Him divine honors; He did not reprove the doubting Thomas, who, after the required proof had been given, cried out, " My Lord and my God." Christ would have refused all this if He were not God, as Paul and Barnabas rejected the divine honors offered to them at Athens.

THE DIVINITY OF CHRIST.

Christ taught His own divinity. He declares Himself greater than Moses, than the prophets, than John the Baptist; He claims the power of forgiving sin, and transmits that power to others; He speaks with His own authority; He foretells coming events, because He knows all things; He reads men's secret thoughts; He acknowledges that He is the Son of God when appealed to solemnly by the High Priest: ." And the high priest said to Him, I adjure thee by the living God, that thou tell us if thou be Christ, the Son of God. Jesus said to him: Thou hast said it" (Math. xxvi. 63, 64). The Jews understood Him by this expression to claim that He was God, not because He possessed reason and intelligence in a high degree, not because He was endowed with eminent sanctity, but because He was in every way the equal of God the Father. He rejected not their understanding of His words; He confirmed it by His death. "The Jews answered him (Pilate), we have a law, and according to the law He ought to die, because He made himself the Son of God" (xix. 7). Jesus Christ has pledged us His word that He is God, and His testimony is true. He is a trustworthy witness, for no sane man will believe that He was deceived, and no one will have the hardihood to assert, in the light of a life so obviously honest, that He wished to deceive others.

Christ's disciples declared His divinity. All the Evangelists teach it. There are four other writers of the New Testament—Peter, Paul, James, and Jude. All these, even Jude in his brief epistle of one chapter, teach the divinity of our Lord. It was taught throughout the entire early Church, so that when Arius denied it in the fourth century he had scarcely a friend in the hierarchy.

Christ's credentials are the miracles which He wrought, and the prophecies which He uttered. The former attest His divinity, since none but God can work a miracle, and the historical evidence alone of the Gospel narratives places these miracles beyond all doubt. Prophecies also prove His divinity, for none but God possesses the habitual gift of looking into the future and there reading of things contingent. Julian, the Apostate, tried to rebuild the Temple, in order to falsify the prophecy: "Behold your house shall be left you desolate." But history records the fact that the Galilean conquered. His prophecies have been tried in the bitterest crucible and have stood the test of centuries.

Christ did not destroy, but absorbed all that was good in Judaism. His life is ineffaceably wrought into the nobler social conceptions of the world. He enforced lessons of morality with a power and a beauty which had then no parallel, and which have since had no revival. Christ is greater than any conqueror the world has ever seen, because He is divine, and that in the highest sense. The rapid spread of the teaching of Mohammed is no more marvelous than the fleet conquests of Alexander or Napoleon. Mohammed and Mohammedans conquered by the sword; Christ and Christians triumphed by the Cross. It is because of the divinity of Christ that the effects of His life on earth are so much more abiding than the results of the greatest conquerors, the systems of the profoundest philosophers, or the teachings of other religious founders.

CHAPTER IV.

MIRACLES.

EVEN though the impiety of some had never exerted itself to make people disbelieve in miracles and thus to set aside one of the positive marks of revelation, and a leading proof of Christianity, yet this subject has sufficient interest and indeed utility to engage our attention. Cardinal Newman points out that the consideration of miracles helps to banish ideas of Fate and Necessity, has a tendency to rouse conscience, to awaken a sense of responsibility, to remind of duty, and to direct attention to those marks of divine government already contained in the ordinary course of events. We talk of the miracles of Lourdes; of the miracles of the Old and New Testament; of the miracles wrought by this or that saint; of the miracles required for the beatification of the blessed or for the canonization of the sainted; to say nothing of the higher object of certain miracles, namely, as evidences of revealed religion, all of which circumstances clothe the subject with not a little interest.

A miracle supposes the existence of God, and is no argument to one who is on principle an Atheist. It is hardly necessary, in order to get an idea of what a miracle is, to go back to first principles and prove the existence of a Supreme Being, a fact abundantly evident from this, that things exist, for otherwise how could they begin to be? From the clock-work order of the universe, for you may as reasonably expect a watch without a watchmaker as this universe with all its complicated machinery without a Creator; from the unanimous consent of all nations acknowledging in some way a Supreme Being, for how otherwise could this idea be stamped upon the minds and hearts of all peoples?

God, and God alone, can work a miracle, for it is something done above, or beyond, or against the order of created nature. Everything that has been created, the material as well as the spiritual, the human soul as well as the earth, goes to make up what is called created nature. God gave to His handiwork a certain force or energy; the use of that energy is action, the need of using it according to rule is law, and the perceptible result from energy so applied is order. In all creation there is a certain order; the same causes in the same circumstances produce the same effects. When a miracle is worked, nature's laws are said to be set aside, or are suspended, or better is it to say superseded, for a higher power is brought to bear upon them. Jesus raised Lazarus from the dead. Nature could not give life to the dead body of Lazarus; it was altogether beyond its power to give life thus. The hand of the miracle-worker was required to do it.

The very essence of a miracle demands that it be in some sense a violation of the laws of nature, and that it be the work of God. Hence, the creation of a human soul and its mysterious union with and workings in the body; hence, even the justification of the sinner, a thing greater than the creation of heaven and earth, are not miracles, for they take place according to a certain uniform course of nature. Hence, also, the works of the angels, be they angels of light or angels of darkness, are not miracles. Hence, again, when we say miracles have been wrought at the shrine of this or that saint, or at those places made sacred by our Blessed Lord, during His life on earth, or by relics, we mean nothing more than this, that God, in order to reward the faith of the people, or for some other reason known to Himself, intervenes and works these miracles in their regard. And when we hear of miracles attributed to the saints, or to the beatified, or to certain pious souls whose names are not enrolled on the calendar of saints, nothing more is meant than that they have been instruments in God's hands of miracle-working, or perhaps they have been the moral causes; that is, by their prayers and good works they moved God to the performance of them.

Some miracles are of a higher order than others. This we find fully illustrated in the miracles of the Gospel. Christ cures the ruler's son who is at the point of death, and the man who has been languishing for thirty-eight years. These are miracles, but not of as high an order as the restoration to life of the widow's son, or of the daughter of Jairus, or of Lazarus; or as the resurrection of Jesus Christ Himself.

There are also miracles of the moral order, as an example of which I should mention the successful energy and perfect unity of the Catholic Church through so many ages. No merely human agency can account for the wonderful spread of the Catholic Church through such weak instruments as a dozen or so of men for the most part unlettered, against obstacles that, humanly speaking, were insurmountable. This is all the more obvious when we consider that the teachings of the Church have penetrated the innermost recesses of the heart; have allayed the pride and prejudices and fierce passions of humanity; have brought to unity men of different nationalities, and languages, and customs, and modes of thought, and philosophies; have reduced to their sway the effeminate courtier and the proud philosopher as well as the more pliant peasant; have made the members of that Church show a zeal and practice austerities hitherto unknown in the world; and made them suffer and die in hundreds of thousands during the persecutions under the Roman emperors.

The question of the possibility of miracles is for us Catholics an easy one. For the Vatican Council has defined: "If any one shall say that miracles can not be wrought, or that they can never be recognized with certainty as such, or that the divine origin of the Christian faith is not rightly proved by miracles, let him be anathema." The Gospels and the Acts of the Apostles narrate events which are clearly miraculous. If we had no well-authenticated miraculous events to tell us of their possibility, we know from the All-powerfulness of God Himself that they can take place, because by virtue of that divine attribute God can do all things that do not involve a contradiction. Even unbelievers do not always go to the length of denying the possibility of miracles. "If you ask me," writes Tyndall in his "Fragments of Science," "who is to limit the outgoings of Almighty Power, my answer is, not I. If you should urge that if the Builder and Maker of this universe chose to stop the rotation of the earth—there is nothing to prevent Him from doing so—I am not prepared to contradict you. It is a subject of which I know nothing." Huxley puts it still more pointedly when he says : " It is and always has been a favorite tenet of mine that Atheism is as absurd, logically speaking, as Polytheism. Denying the possibility of miracles seems to me quite as unjustifiable as speculative Atheism." Renan and Rousseau are equally explicit. The latter becomes indignant that any one should question whether or not God can derogate from the laws which He Himself has established, and declares the subject, if seriously treated, would be impious, if not absurd. Surely the Creator of force and matter can also annihilate them, and if He can annihilate them, there is nothing unreasonable in holding that He can modify them.

From a Christian point of view, miracles have more value than at first blush we may be inclined to give them. They are decisive proofs of the truth of any doctrine in favor of which they may have been wrought. For God alone can work a miracle. " Praise the Lord, for He is good, for His mercy endureth for ever. Who alone doth great wonders, for His mercy endureth for ever" (Psalm cxxxv. 1–4). A miracle is simply the voice of God. When He fed the Israelites with manna it was as plainly and as eloquently the voice of God as if He had come down from Heaven and preached a panegyric on the virtue of charity. The fiery serpents expressed God's wrath as clearly as did His words when He said, "I will destroy this stiff-necked people." Even man can express his thoughts in many ways. There is a language of the eye, and of the brow, and of the cheek, and of the arm, as well as of the tongue. And sometimes it is more expressive than the spoken word. Miracles are the speech of God, and when worked to prove anything, are God's eloquence in favor of the truth of that thing.

But to come down more to particulars. The miracles worked by our Lord prove to demonstration the divinity of the Christian religion, for, as we have seen, they are God's evidence of its truth. These miracles are narrated in the historical books of the New Testament. Passing by for the moment the inspired authority of the sacred narratives, all must admit their historical worth. All must give to them that amount of credence which they can not withhold from a respectable book of history. And this, because they are genuine, and bear the stamp of integrity and veracity. The fathers and other writers, even non-Catholics, give evidence that they were written by those whose names they bear, and about the time they claim to have been written. Nor could anyone else write these books and hope with success to attribute them to the Apostles. No Jew or heathen would attribute such miracles to Christ as the Gospels speak of, and if they or anyone else did write these books and then falsely say that they were the effusions of the Apostles, a remonstrance loud and long should have been heard, but of this there is not a single trace. For this reason, also, as well as for others, we know that these miracle-narratives have come down to us free from any substantial change.

They bear about them all the evidences of fact. Some of the writers were eye-witnesses and ear-witnesses to the facts of which they wrote. The facts were public, obvious, done sometimes under their very eyes, at different times and places, fraught with the greatest consequences, of the utmost importance in themselves, as also by reason of the object for which they were accomplished. Names of persons, and places, and dates, are given, so that if fraud existed it could be easily detected. People do not practice deception unless they expect some benefit. For a greater reason they do not deceive, if, as a result, they may expect poverty, persecution, and death. And if they wished to deceive they could not do so ; because the facts were too public, too grave, too opposed to the prejudices of the people, having for their object the subversion of tenets consecrated by time-honored custom, and the propagation of a religion hateful to the people and their ruler, so detested that they put its founder, Jesus Christ, to death.

Christ came on earth to establish a religion, and He proved by miracles that Christianity is from God. He showed that He was Lord of inanimate creation by changing water into wine, by calming the sea and the tempest, and by feeding the hungry multitude with the multiplied loaves and fishes. He further showed His divine mission by another class of miracles, by curing the sick sometimes by touch, sometimes by command, sometimes the near, sometimes the absent and far-distant. More marvelous still are the life-restoring miracles, such as took place in the case of the daughter of the chief of the synagogue, of the son of the widow of Naim, and of Lazarus, the brother of Martha and Mary.

But the crowning proof of the divinity of Christianity is to be found in Christ's resurrection. The four Gospels give us an account of the death of Christ, and whilst differing in many little circumstances, which point to the truthfulness and independence of the narratives, they do not contradict each other in one single iota. They tell us of the various incidents which led up to the crucifixion; the hatred of the Jewish priests and princes, the arrest of Christ, the various judicial proceedings against Him, His condemnation, and the feeble efforts of Pontius Pilate to secure His release. They tell us of the number of witnesses at His death. There were John, the beloved disciple, the Blessed Virgin Mary, the other holy women, the Roman soldiers in charge of the prisoners, the centurion in command, the high-priests and scribes, the vast concourse of people who went out to see the spectacle; so that if all these were deceived it would have been a miracle more miraculous than the resurrection itself.

The hatred of the Jewish officials made them be cautious not to deliver up the body of Christ until they were certain that He was dead—a fact which, as Renan confesses, is of itself sufficient to prove the actuality of His death. The piercing of His side by the Roman soldier, from which blood and water flowed, is proof of Christ's death as great as is the incredulity of Thomas of His resurrection. Thomas refused to believe in a risen Saviour until he had seen the marks of the instruments of the crucifixion. The unbelief of St. Thomas is, according to St. Gregory the Great, more profitable unto faith than the faith of the believing disciple. Christ's body was placed in a tomb hollowed out of a rock, the door was sealed with the public seal, a large stone was placed upon it, and soldiers kept guard lest the disciples should come and steal away the body, and say Christ had arisen. In addition to all these precautions there is the amplest testimony of His resurrection. The witnesses are Mary Magdalene, the other women to whom Christ appeared, the two disciples on their way to Emaus, eleven Apostles and more than five hundred brethren. They saw Him again and again, at home and abroad, in the city and out of it; they talked with Him, they heard the sound of His voice, they touched Him on invitation; so that they had the same means of knowing that Christ had arisen as they had of the existence of the world around them. It is on this miracle—the resurrection of Christ, proved by most trustworthy and accumulative evidence from the historical books of the New Testament—that we base a leading proof of the divinity of the Christian religion. Apart altogether from the question of inspiration and from the Vatican definition, we have a moral certainty that miracles have taken place. When Christ said: "Take up thy bed and walk," and when He said, "Lazarus, come forth," He showed that they are not the result of strange and unknown laws of nature. It is not necessary, in order to know whether or not something is miraculous, to know well the laws of nature, to be versed in geology and astronomy, to talk glibly of the tertiary period, to be able to find the altitude of the sun at noon, to speak learnedly of logarithms, to measure the velocity of sound, and such like excellent things in their way.

Every man, lettered or unlettered, rude or cultured, the woodman of St. Thomas Aquinas or the courtier of Whitehall, will tell you that to change water into wine, and to raise the dead to life, are miracles.

Even yet there are miracles in the Church of God; even yet there are such things as ecclesiastical miracles. There is not the same necessity for miracles now as in the days of the Apostles, yet there is no antecedent improbability against their continuation. Nations are still to be converted. The Jewish religion was well established during the lifetime of Moses, nevertheless God worked miracles afterwards for that stiff-necked and ungrateful people. A certain Catholic writer well sums up the present aspect of the question in this way: " The more profoundly and extensively we consider the intimate union of Christ with the Church, and His unspeakable, inconceivable love for her, manifested in such and so many ways, the less improbable would it appear, antecedent to all accounts of the fact, that He would work miracles; in one place to quicken and reward the piety of the faithful; in another to terrify or persuade them to repentance; in another to mark His special love for His devoted servants; in another to testify to the sanctity and confirm the authority of those whom He destines for some great work in the Church, as in the case of St. Thomas of Aquin, or St. Ignatius, or St. Philip Neri, or St. Theresa, or St. Alphonsus Liguori; or whom He destines for a consolation to the Church, or for an example of some one virtue, or of all virtues in the heroic degree, as in the case of St. Aloysius or St. Mary Magdalen of Pazzis." And when ecclesiastical authority speaks we are bound to show our filial respect, and when the Church proclaims the actuality of miracles, as she does in the case of beatification and canonization, it would be presumptuous on our part to withhold our assent.

We have seen that Christ proved the divinity of Christianity by miracles. Christianity and Catholicity are convertible terms. Our faith is the same to-day as when Christ proved its truth before an unsympathetic audience, or when St. Paul spread the light before

Athenian heathens; for we are told that the gates of hell shall not prevail against the Church, and Christ promised to remain always with it. And if superstition and imposture, by way of pretended miracles, occasionally accompanied the propagation of Christianity, though they might obscure, they could not conceal the true work of God in His Church, of which work they were but the mockery.

CHAPTER V.

FAITH AND REASON.

THE eleventh chapter of the Epistle of St. Paul to the Hebrews is for Faith, what the famous thirteenth chapter of his first letter to the Corinthians is for Charity. In it the Apostle does not define, but rather describes, Faith when he says, it is the "substance of things to be hoped for, the evidence of things that appear not." By Faith we mean belief on the authority of another. If that other be a human witness, then the Faith is human; if divine, then the Faith is divine. The difference between them is well pointed out by Cardinal Newman in the following words: "Divine Faith is assenting to a doctrine as true, because God says it is true, Who cannot lie. And farther than this; since God says it is true, not with His own voice, but by the voice of His messengers, it is assenting to what man says, not simply viewed as a man, but to what he is commissioned to declare, as a messenger, prophet, or ambassador from God. In the ordinary course of this world we account things true, either because we see them, or we can perceive that they follow and are deducible from what we do see; that is, we gain truth by sight or by reason, not by Faith. You will say, indeed, that we accept a number of things which we can not prove or see, on the word of others; certainly : but then we accept what they say only as the word of man; and we have not commonly that absolute and unreserved confidence in them which nothing can shake. We know that man is open to mistake, and we are always glad to find some confirmation of what he says from other quarters, in any important matter; or we receive his information with negligence and unconcern, as something of little consequence as a matter of opinion; or, if we act upon it, it is a matter of prudence, thinking it safest and best to do so. We take his word for what it is worth, and we use it according to our necessity, or its probability. We keep the decision in our hands, and reserve the right of reöpening the question whenever we please. This is very different from divine Faith; he who believes that God is true, and that this is His word which He has committed to man, has no doubt at all. He is as certain that the doctrine taught is true, as that God is true; and he is certain, because God is true, because God has spoken, not because he sees its truth, or can prove its truth. That is, Faith has two peculiarities: it is most certain, decided, positive, and immovable assent; and it gives this assent, not because it sees with eye, or sees with reason, but because it receives the tidings from one that comes from God."

Faith, as it exists in the mind, is interior; when manifested by words or signs, it is called exterior Faith. And this division is very different from implicit and explicit Faith. For it is implicit when we believe, in a general way, truth unknown to us in particular; and it is explicit when the truths we believe are clearly known to us. Our theologians make another distinction. They tell us that Faith is living when it is animated by sanctifying grace, and dead when no such grace accompanies it. To this distinction St. Paul refers when he speaks of "Faith working by Charity," in opposition to "Faith without works, which is dead."

Faith bridges the gulf between the world of time and the world of eternity; and if I were asked, What does it believe? I should simply say, it believes the Word of God, that is, His whole revelation. This revelation is made in the face of nature, in the things created by which His existence is proved, in the lights of our intellect and the dictates of our conscience. Thus far there is question of what we may call the natural Word of God. There is also a supernatural Word—the Word which came through the prophets, the revelation on Pentecost, that which we received through the coming of God the Son on earth, and all that He taught, the things of which He spoke when He said, "I have many things to say to you, but you can not hear them now." Holy Scripture is the written Word of God; the unwritten Word is the living Scripture, which is stamped upon the "world-wide and lineal intelligence of the Church."

The *wherefore*, or motive, for our belief, is the veracity of God. The Christian revelation has been established by miracles, and the historical evidence of this fact is as strong and as accessible as the grounds for belief in the existence of Julian the Apostate. Knowing this, we know it is God who speaks, and since He is infinite wisdom, He can not be deceived. Hence the mind yields a firm assent to revealed doctrine, on the authority of God Himself. From this, it is clear that the motive of credibility is quite different from the motive of Faith. The motive of credibility is the reason or evidence why we believe a doctrine to be revealed; the motive of Faith is the reason why we give assent to that doctrine.

A truth of Faith may be evident in itself, and the same truth may be known by reason as well as by revelation. Such, for example, is the existence of God. Nature tells us of a Supreme Being, Scripture tells us of a living God. It is not opinion, and does not admit of doubt; for the proofs of a Christian revelation are decisive, and the evidences of an infallible authority in the Church are certain. There can not be a doctrine of Divine Faith, unless it be revealed, and as circumstances demand, the Church proposes for our acceptance, dogmas of Faith. Thus the Divinity of Christ, whilst always a matter of Divine Faith, was not formally proposed to the faithful until the Council of Nice, held in the year 325 in order to crush the Arian heresy. To come down to our time, the doctrines of Papal Infallibility and of the Immaculate Conception always belonged to Divine Faith, but it was not until the Vatican Council that the former was solemnly and formally put before us, whilst the latter was defined by Pio Nono in the year 1854.

All Christians, whilst not agreeing as to the nature of Faith, are at one with regard to its necessity for salvation. They teach with St. Paul that "without Faith it is impossible to please God" (Heb. xi. 6); and with Christ, "He that believeth not shall be condemned" (Luke xvi. 16). Faith is a grace, and grace assists but does not destroy nature. Without the gift of God no one can have Faith; it belongs not to the order in which we are born. It is given to every baptized infant, and, as Cardinal Manning points out, it is just as possible for the unconscious infant to have the gift of Faith as it is for the unconscious infant to have the gift of reason. The difficulty to believe does not come from opposition between faith and reason, but from opposition between man's will and God's grace.

So far from being opposed to reason, it is eminently reasonable. We believe in the mysteries of nature, because ample testimony convinces us that they exist. We believe in the mysteries of Faith, because still more unexceptionable evidence proves their existence—the evidence of Christ and His Church. It is unreasonable to assent to any proposition without evidence. We are told of an Indian prince who never saw ice, but heard of its existence on trustworthy authority. He would have been unreasonable if he had refused to believe. We give assent to truths of Faith, not on human authority, but on evidence that is divine. Reason can and ought to lead us up to the very porch of Faith. Yet Faith does not come from reason, and is not an extension of it. Mechanical power may aid the hearing or the sight, or the other senses, as the telephone aids the sense of hearing and the telescope the sense of sight, still the same natural faculties remain. And so with reason, however extended, it does not give us Faith. When we speak of reason as distinguished from Faith, we mean the whole collection of mental faculties and the principles discovered by them. Each has its own province. There are limits beyond which reason can not go in the discovery of truth. Time, space, causation, matter, light, sound, electricity, and the rest, have each and all their mysteries. It is not wonderful, then, that Bayle said his life was passed in the midst of mysteries.

There is another means of communicating truths not

discoverable by reason, and that we call revelation. If we admit the existence of God, we can not deny His power of communicating truths to us. Still more, the history of humanity and the history of philosophy show the necessity of such a revelation; for, in its absence the world was steeped in the grossest forms of error and philosophy was unable to remedy the common ignorance of mankind.

There is a twofold harmony between Faith and reason. One is of a negative nature, because it shows there is no opposition between them ; the other is positive, for it shows that revelation opens up a wide field of speculation for reason, and it shows how the latter helps to Faith. There is no opposition to reason in those revealed truths which reason itself can discern ; there is no opposition in these truths which reason can not reach. Reason helps to Faith, because it shows that there is a limit to its own powers ; it shows that revelation is possible and even necessary ; it shows and examines the evidences of revealed truth ; and having accepted the revelation, it can show the reasonableness of the doctrine itself.

Reason can demonstrate the possibility and actual truth of certain doctrines which we can not *comprehend*. For we can understand a truth without being able to comprehend it, that is, we may know its meaning without being able to account for it; without being able to show how the subject and attribute can be united or separated as stated in the proposition. Reason, then, is not an obstacle but an aid to belief. Between the fulness of Faith and the hollowness of unbelief there is an inclined plane on which, if people struggle not upward, they descend rapidly. Protestantism is no longer one of the competing creeds. The battle is between Catholicity and unbelief. The Via Media has been tried and found wanting. "I came to the conclusion," writes Cardinal Newman, "that there is no medium in true philosophy between Atheism and Catholicity, and that a perfectly consistent mind, under these circumstances in which it finds itself here below, must embrace either one or the other." And the grand old historic Church, great and respected (as a famous English essayist points out) before the Saxon had set foot on Britain, before the French had crossed the Rhine, when Grecian eloquence still flourished in Antioch, when idols were still worshiped in the temple of Mecca, will go on living and doing good in spite of the newest Reformation.

CHAPTER VI.

FAITH AND PHYSICS.

IN the foregoing chapter we explained what Faith is, its motive, its object, and the harmony between it and reason; in this we shall confine our remarks to Faith and Physics, or physical science. If we stop to consider that apostasy is the most heinous of all sins, it is worth our while to give some thought to one of its chiefest causes. Besides what may be called the moral causes of loss of Faith,—such as indiscreet marriage, bad books, errors in life,—there is another wide-spread cause, and it is misapprehension of the scope of physical science. Mark well, the cause is not too much knowledge, but too little. The more nebulous the intellect, the more likely it is to reject Faith. Ruskin's words on Darwin throw some light on the idea we wish to impress. The great art-critic writes: "Darwin has a mortal fascination for all vainly curious and speculative persons, and has collected in the train of him every impudent imbecile in Europe, like a dim comet wagging its useless tail of phosphorescent light across the steadfast stars." Biology and not religion, was the study of the learned author of the "Origin of Species." But, like the mischief wrought by the imitators of Carlyle in literature, the weak followers of Darwin work sad havoc through the instrumentality of theories that might well be Christianized. And so with the other branches of physical science.

Physics treats of the science of nature, or of natural objects, comprehending the study of the natural world. Physics deals with matter only. Its province is very narrow. It deals not with final destiny, nor with essence, or first cause, but takes things as we find them. Science, as distinguished from art, inquires for the sake of knowledge; art, for the sake of production. Art lays down certain rules; science demonstrates the truth of these rules. It is a popular error to restrict the word "scientist" to the student of physical science. Theology, for example, treating as it does of God and the things which belong to Him, is as much a science as is the study of natural phenomena.

Verily we need a new Theology, or rather a Theology accommodated to meet the phases of the age. "We were believers," writes Jules Simon, "we have become sceptics, to-morrow we shall be nihilists." Scripture is no longer of much use in controversy, except from a historical point of view. We do not require it as a defense against Protestantism, for Protestantism no longer protests. What little remains of it is a fragmentary Christianity, a "serviceable break-water against doctrinal errors more fundamental than its own," and therefore it is idle to wage a Scriptural warfare against it while scepticism in all its forms grows more aggressive.

In days gone by, the fiercest form of attack was made upon the Church in the name of Metaphysics; now it is made in the name of Physics. If we face the question squarely and ask ourselves, are the revelations of Christianity really at variance with the facts of Physics?

we can answer, without fear, that there is not a single case where a certain contradiction has been discovered. Facts of physical science are few, hypotheses many. We ought to distinguish what is certain in physical science from what is merely probable, and we should never forget that the many wrecked hypotheses of that branch would make a very large volume. And it is of moment to keep this before the mind's eye, because mere theories are so often set forward by the shallow and flippant as facts, and we are asked, with a flourish of trumpets, either to reconcile them with the certain truths of Christianity, or to surrender the latter at discretion. Even Charles Darwin did not put forward evolution as anything more than a theory, but cloudy imitators have done the rest, and have rushed in where he, with all his wealth of learning, feared to tread. Students of physical science have been at work against Christianity for a long time, and we have no evidence that they have found for a certainty any flaw in it.

In the early ages of Christianity, the Gnostics, with their strange mixture of oriental theology and Greek philosophy, and some doctrines of Christianity, professed to explain everything by the light of reason. Now a large number of those who are antagonistic to Christ's teaching call themselves Agnostics, professing to know nothing about the supernatural.

It is a strange principle to start out with, that Faith and physical science are in opposition. One truth may run parallel with another, or even on a higher plane, but can never be opposed to it. The same God who gives the grace of Faith, gives light for the discovery of the facts of physical science. Scientists have no right to ask us to reconcile mere theories with Christianity. Hypotheses are but hypothetical facts, if we may use the expression; and if we take away these, there will be very few scientific facts remaining. All scientific facts we admit in advance; we promote research and its results please us. It is in strict conformity with Christianity to say that all known facts, and all facts yet undiscovered, are in harmony with the Christian religion. Revelation is the basis of Faith, and even Renan and Strauss admit, when urged, that revelation is an acknowledged historical fact. Dogma may destroy many hypotheses, but it does not stand between physics and facts.

If we look upon science by reason of its object, it forms into two great divisions—supernatural and natural. The object of supernatural science is God. That part of natural science which treats of intellectual and moral truths, belongs to Metaphysics. The domain of Physics is therefore very limited, being restricted to purely material phenomena. The lowest in the order of sciences is Physics; the highest, Theology. This needs no proof beyond the consideration of the object of each science. Ask yourself, What is the object of Theology? and what is the object of Physics? and the answers show how immeasurably superior the former is to the latter. Even as compared with Metaphysics, physical science stands low. Dealing merely with sensible phenomena, it is as far below Metaphysics as sight is below intelligence. We are not finding fault; we are merely pointing out the scope of physical science. To our mind it is as reasonable to find fault with an ass for not being a horse, as to find fault with physical science because it can not examine and solve, according to its own methods, questions of Metaphysics and Theology. But we do take it to be an evidence of intellectual poverty, when we find physicists undertaking to solve, either in a negative or a positive way, by the methods and principles of physical science, questions that belong entirely to the region of Metaphysics or of Theology.

For the sake of clearness, we must distinguish between two schools, the positivist and the materialistic. The first says that questions of final cause and first cause, and origin and substance, are entirely unknowable to us. It assigns as a reason that these are outside the pale of observation by the senses. We answer, If they present no phenomena for the senses, then you are not justified in pronouncing them unknowable. All you can justly say, is that they are unknowable by the principles of your science, and as your science is very limited, perhaps they are knowable by the principles of higher sciences. Even if they are outside the pale of observation by the senses, they are not therefore outside the pale of perception by our reason. The materialistic school of science undertakes to decide all questions, whether physical, metaphysical, or religious. This is monstrous. Why should they attempt to do so, if questions of Metaphysics and Theology be not regulated by a code of laws founded on material phenomena?

Even in matters outside the province of physical science, the physicists will accept no proofs and no methods but their own. Here they lay themselves open to the charge of holding a fragmentary teaching of a half-educated school. "It is no taunt," writes Mr. Mallock, "it is simply the statement of a biological fact, to say that a large number of physicists have been so imperfectly educated in the very rudiments of philosophy as hardly to realize what there is to be accounted for. They accept their external world as a savage does, or as an English agricultural laborer does." Thus it is lack of education and want of knowledge which cause this apparent collision of Faith and Physics.

The logic of scientific and sociological moralists rejects dogmas of Faith as unnecessary, if not hostile, to the highest life. Whilst we know that the earth is but an atom in the awful vastness of the universe, yet their appeal is rather to the imagination than to reason. Let me again quote that most fascinating of modern philosophers—W. H. Mallock—whose words show there is nothing shocking to the scientific imagination in all those questions of Faith wound up in the teaching that the earth is the abode of a special race ennobled by a Redeemer : " The selection of this one small planet as the abode of a race special and so preëminent as the Incarnation and Redemption would argue man to be, the selection of this earth, in fact, as the spiritual centre of all things, is an idea which, properly considered, is far less shocking to the scientific imagination than it seems to be. It is indeed strictly in accordance with the doctrines of evolution and natural selection. Everything in the world around us that comes to maturity is produced by a process of what seems to be a boundless waste. What innumerable ages have gone to the making of man! What innumerable ova are wasted for any one thing that lives ! In the same way, what myriads and myriads of stars may be wasted and lifeless, whilst this one has received the God of Gods upon it ! * * * I only wish to affirm that when the time for the struggle comes the imagination that affirms may be more than a match for the imagination that denies."

Certain leaders of modern thought try to impress upon us that the study of nature, or physical science, leads away from God. Common sense and a little philosophy teach, with St. Paul, that we learn of God from His works, that we look "from nature up to nature's God." The Psalmist taught the same: "The heavens show forth the glory of God, and the firmament declareth the work of His hands" (Ps. xviii. 2). The words of the Vatican Council, as explaining the apparent conflict between Faith and Physical science, have almost become commonplace in the writings of churchmen: "There never can be any real discrepancy between reason and Faith, since the same God who reveals mysteries has bestowed the light of reason on the human mind; and God can not deny Himself, nor can truth ever contradict truth. The false appearance of such a contradiction is mainly due either to dogmas of Faith not having been clearly understood and expounded according to the mind of the Church, or to the inventions of opinion having been taken for the verdict of reason." We should not forget that there is a natural and a supernatural revelation of the mind of God. God has formally spoken to man. Christianity teaches that "God, at sundry times and in divers manners, spoke in times past to the Fathers by the Prophets, last of all; in these days hath spoken to us by His Son." Theology, or the highest science, treats of this manifestation of the Almighty. God also reveals Himself by the visible powers of nature. Physical science deals with this latter. We may compare science and religion to the sisters Martha and Mary. They are daughters of the same Father. They minister to the same Lord, but in a different way. Science, like Martha, is busy about material things.

Religion, like Mary, is kneeling at the feet of her Lord.

It is strange that such men as are represented by Herbert Spencer, should foster the impression that Christianity is hostile to physical science; and, that physicists as such, continually run the risk of having an ecclesiastical ukase directed against them. They tell us our articles of Faith are hindrances upon scientific research. We answer: knowledge of any kind defines truth, and therefore limits inquiry. Let us illustrate our meaning. Suppose we learn on unexceptionable authority that the bison is not to be found in any State east of the Mississippi, we should act unwisely were we to search Illinois, or Ohio, or New York for that animal.

They appeal with triumphant scorn to the case of Galileo. Nicholas Cosa, a humble but learned priest, in a work on Astronomy, written well-nigh two hundred years before Galileo, taught the heliocentric system. The representatives of Christianity did not condemn him, but Pope Nicholas the Fifth gave him a Cardinal's hat by way of compliment. Copernicus, a professor in the Pope's University, taught the same thing and enraptured an audience of two thousand students by his lectures on the new astronomical theory. Rome also favored him, and on his retirement he received a life pension. But they kept religion apart from their philosophical speculations. Galileo dragged in the Scriptures most incontinently. The purpose of the Sacred Scriptures is not to teach astronomy; and if here and there we find astronomical references which are not scientifically correct, we must remember that the inspired writer was only making use of popular language to teach a lesson, in the same way as we speak of sunrise and sunset, though, as a matter of fact, the sun neither rises nor sets. Galileo's theory could not be proved to a certainty until the velocity of light and its aberrations, and the laws of gravitation were established.

Nor were Catholic prelates the only ones who resented this misuse of the Scriptures, and were in apparent opposition to the progress of physical science. Thirty years before Galileo got into trouble, the astronomer Kepler was condemned by the Protestant theological faculty of Tubingen. After much vexatious treatment, he, staunch Protestant to the last, fled to Jesuits of Gratez and Ingoldstadt for protection. What is the use of saying that the *Church*, without knowing it, taught officially or *ex cathedra* in the Galileo case? One might as well say a man can commit a formal sin without knowing it. The Galileo case impresses this upon us, that theologians should not disregard the scientific teaching of their age. Let us suppose that the Roman Congregation which condemned Galileo was at fault, what follows? No harm, that we know of, befalls the Church or any of her doctrines. Catholics never said that Roman Congregations were infallible. The fact of a mistake having been made in Galileo's case, neither retards nor accelerates the progress of science, but it does emphasize the truth that infallibility rests not with sacred congregations, but with the Church and with the Pope, in matters of faith and morals, when teaching *ex cathedra.*

The very mission of the Church requires the promotion of science. Her mission is to the scientist as well as to the savage. Her missionaries must learn the technical terminology of the former as well as the rude and undeveloped language of the latter.

The grand and simple laws of nature have no terrors for Christianity. The most honored names in every department of physical science are those of Catholics. It was a French ecclesiastic, Picard, who made the first accurate measurement of a degree of the meridian, and thus enabled Newton to establish the principle of universal gravitation; Peter Angelo Secchi, an Italian Jesuit, was the greatest student of the sun who ever lived, and has written the best work upon it; Pope Gregory the Thirteenth settled the hitherto all-confusing question of chronology; Balboa, a Spanish Catholic, enriched geography by being the first to catch sight of the Pacific Ocean, and Magellan, a Portuguese Catholic, still further enlarged that science by being the first to sail around the earth. To Catholics we are indebted for our knowledge of the three laws of motion, the basis of modern mechanical science. A Venetian friar, Luca Borgo, wrote the first European work on algebra; Pascal, a Catholic, aided Leibnitz in the invention of the differential calculus; and one of the greatest names in optics is Augustin Jean Fresnel. Fizeau, a Catholic, first measured the velocity of light, and the experiments of Galvani, another Catholic, were the beginning of dynamic electricity. Lavoisier was the founder of modern chemistry, and the most distinguished name in mineralogy is that of René Just Haug. Even in geology, that newest branch of physical science, which testifies to the truth of the sacred record of Genesis, we find such Catholics as Da Vinci, Friscatores, and the Danish bishop, Nicholaus Stans, holding prominent places.

The admission of the supernatural will go a great way towards reconciling religion and science. If we bear in mind that physical science is not the only science, that its scope is comparatively limited, that its methods and principles are not intended for questions of Theology and Metaphysics; if we remember what physical science owes to Catholic physicists; if we recall to mind the history of the Church in relation to this science, then Faith and Physics are easily harmonized.

CHAPTER VII.

FAITH AND EVOLUTION.

EVOLUTION still continues to be the watchword of advanced scholarship. It is not our purpose to offer anything new on this subject, but rather to give, in a short and easy form, the teaching of some writers. We shall treat the question principally in reference to the creation of man. Though all do not agree as to what Evolution is, yet there is sufficient agreement to enable us to trace its general outlines. It implies a common ancestry.. All living things, it tells us, are united in some way by ties of relationship. Charles Darwin points out a strong resemblance between certain forms of animal and vegetable life. He says that life commenced in some simplest forms, and gradually became more complex till man appeared. It would seem that the parable of the mustard-seed is the parable of creation, and that man's body is a résumé of the lower beings. According to that most painstaking scientist, natural selection, or the survival of the fittest, directs and in some way controls this Evolution. The phrase, natural selection, is taken in contradistinction to artificial selection. By artificial selection man produces the dog from the wolf and the white rose from the red. Natural selection is the power which preserves species against adverse influences by utilizing the individual peculiarities favorable to their existence, and by cutting off all such peculiarities as are not favorable. In justice to the great scientist, he nowhere maintains that he has completely proved his theories.

Though Huxley and Spencer are not quite satisfied with Darwin's Evolution, yet the lesser lights accept it in all its simple grandeur. Whilst Kant, Laplace, and Erasmus Darwin were the real founders of modern Evolution, Charles Darwin is beyond doubt its high-priest.

Professor Mivart says, Evolution depends on some unknown law. This acts only where there are conditions favorable to Evolution. Then changes are caused so great as to distinguish species from species. Thus man's body was made.

Some find in Evolution an argument for Theism; others, with Frederick Harrison, discover in it a reason for the grossest Materialism. Among all Evolutionists there is this in common—an opposition to the popular belief as regards the creation. Herbert Spencer satirizes the popular idea, and calls belief in a special creation a carpenter-like theory.

Every Christian must hold that God created man. Let us take the description of the creation as given in Genesis. "And He said: Let us make man to our image and likeness; and let him have dominion over the fishes of the sea, and the fowls of the air, and the beasts, and the whole earth, and every creeping creature that moveth upon the earth. And God created man to His own image; to the image of God He created him: male and female He created them" (i. 26, 27). "And the Lord God formed man of the slime of the earth; and breathed into his face the breath of life, and man became a living soul" (ii. 7).

The question therefore for us is, how did God make man? God formed man's body from dust or slime, and breathed into that body a living soul. Evolution can have no place in reference to the soul. The evolution of mind from matter is eminently Atheistic. That the soul of Adam was specially created is a dogma of Catholic Faith. It is also of Faith that the origin of the human soul in each individual of Adam's posterity is not an evolution of organic or of inorganic forms of existence. Moreover, though not formally defined, yet the everyday teaching of the Church seems to make it of Faith, that one soul can not produce another. Hence, we say each individual receives his soul immediately from God as Adam did. Everyone agrees that there is no doctrinal difficulty in admitting Evolution in reference to all organisms lower than man. This, however, does not imply that matter has in itself all the potentiality of terrestrial life, and goes on in its own development alone and by its own energy. The subject, then, is reduced to the manner in which God created man's body. Some few contemplate the possibility of angelic ministration in the formation of man, but this does not materially affect the question.

There are three things which show forth in a marked manner the supreme dominion of the Creator, and the entire dependence of the created. They are: first, creation, or the production of a thing from nothing; second, conservation, or the keeping in existence of the thing created; third, coöperation (concursus), or the influence of the Creator on the creature in order that the latter may act. This coöperation is necessary for all actions. Besides the general coöperation of God, our question as to the manner in which He made man implies an additional act.

Our query may be put in another way, which may make it yet more clear. No evolutionary process can account for man's intellect; no evolutionary process can account for even the beginnings of morality which are to be found in all, even in the most undignified savage. These two thoughts in themselves are enough to prevent our acceptance of the Darwinian theory in its entirety. Leaving the question of the human soul as settled; passing over that of intellect and morality; may we not hold that the body was not formed immediately by God, and that it originated in a lower species? If we maintain that the formation of man's body was not immediate, but rather the result of a long and slow process, then the texts of Genesis, quoted above, must be taken in a sense other than literal. Nor does this present an insuperable difficulty, because, as every student of the inspired word knows, the Scriptures may be taken in many senses. When we read that God breathed into man's face the breath of life, it is evident that the words are not to be accepted in the strictest sense. Why, then, should we be bound to interpret the first half of the same text in its narrowest sense? There is no reason why we should, to be found in the text, nor in the context, nor in any other part of the Sacred Scriptures. If reason there be, it must be from some other source. In addition to the words of Genesis, other texts are also quoted, such as from Job: "Thy hands have made me, and fashioned me wholly round about. Remember, I beseech Thee, that thou hast made me as the clay" (i. 8, 9). It is a common usage of speech to attribute the results of dependent and proximate causes to the principal one. Thus we often hear the phrase, "I built that house," used by the man who merely employed others to do the work. So also the results of the actions of secondary causes are attributed by Sacred Scripture to the immediate action of God.

Professor Mivart, in his "Lessons from Nature," says that the strictest ultramontane is at liberty to hold the doctrine of Evolution. The learned doctor is speaking of what is merely animal in the nature of man. And the origin of man from a lower animal form, is, in reality, a higher origin than from dust or slime. Evolution as a process pervades all nature. We find it in language; we find it in the powers of the mind; we find it in the products of every season and clime. Human life is at present evolved, for it passes through many stages. It does not, therefore, seem so utterly repugnant that Adam's body should have been formed in some such similar way.

It is the soul which ennobles man, and makes him lord of creation. If we state an evident fact, the similarity to be found between man's body and that of some animals, we do not lower him from his high place, because the soul, the distinguishing element, remains untouched. Every creature begins life under a simpler and more different form from that which it afterwards attains. The oak from the acorn, the caterpillar from the egg, are cases in point. Why should the material part of man be an exception?

Nor does there seem to be any decisive reason in the writings of the Fathers against holding Evolution in reference to Adam's body, at least, as a possible hypothesis. St. Augustine, in his work on Genesis, whilst warning us against loquacious philosophy on the one hand, and superstitious timidity on the other, recommends the greatest latitude in the interpretation of obscure passages of Holy Writ. Catholics are well aware of the Tridentine teaching not to interpret the Scriptures contrary to the unanimous consent of the Fathers. In view of the present subject, it is well to bear in mind what is meant by Patristic unanimity of consent, and what the object of that consent must be in order to be decisive. Whilst some quote St. Augustine as holding Evolution to be in harmony with Christian doctrines, it is certain that the whole school of St. Basil, which is nearly the entire *traditio patrum*, teach the immediate formation of man's body by God. We fear, however, the great Doctor of Grace was not a prophet of the future possibilities of science, and the theologians of the school of St. Basil, whilst they meant to exclude Gnostic and Manichean errors and other false theories of the time regarding matter in general and man's body in particular, could hardly be expected to be well versed in a question which has taken shape in comparatively modern times. An example may throw some light on the meaning of the unanimous consent of the Fathers. All of them of any note except St. Augustine hold the six days of creation to be ordinary ones. Nevertheless there is no obligation from Faith binding us to believe that the days of creation were twenty-four hours long, rather than indefinite periods of time. Perhaps, then, the single dissentient voice of the great Latin Father is able to destroy the unanimity of consent. Again, it is suggested that we may distinguish between *material* and *formal* consent. The *material*, "unanimous consent of the Fathers," is when they merely say the same thing; the *formal*, when they use words to the effect that such is the sense, and such alone, in which a certain passage may be taken. With this distinction before our mind, even if the school of St. Basil represented the sense of the Church, may we not say that the unanimity was simply material, and therefore no more obligatory than the unanimous consent regarding the six days of creation? It must be borne in mind throughout, that we are speaking of man's body, not of man. For man did not exist until the human soul was infused into the pre-existing being, whatever that being was, and whenever this action took place. If we suppose, then, the creation of man's body to be a purely scientific question, and not essentially connected with Faith and morals, we are within our right in saying that it is not for a certainty one of these subjects on which the unanimous consent of the Fathers is decisive. The authority of the Fathers extends only to matters of Faith and morals, and truths essentially connected with them. Hence their purely scientific views have no greater value than the scientific principles on which they depend. Evidence and not authority is the direct criterion of scientific truth.

We come now to the teaching of our theologians. Professor Mivart is at fault in calling the consensus of our theologians a bug-bear to timid Catholics. A continuous consensus of Catholic teaching is, as the Vatican Council points out, obligatory on Catholics. It is rash to maintain without at least a probable foundation, an opinion which is opposed to the commonly received teaching of the theologians. But theologians may teach in two ways. They may teach something as their own opinion, or they may teach it as a revealed truth. If in the latter way, then, no doubt, the continuous consensus of the theologians should have some binding force on Catholics. But such does not appear to be the case, if proposed in the former way. Although Dr. Bernard Schafer, Dr. Carl Guettler, Padre Secchi, and other modern theologians, hold the Evolutionary process in reference to Adam's body at least as a possible hypothesis, and Father Harper, with more courage, states, that the principle of natural Evolution is in strict accordance with the teaching of St. Thomas and the Fathers of the Church, yet the majority of theologians taught and teach the immediate creation of Adam's body. But it is by no means clear whether they taught this merely as their own opinion, or whether they taught it as a revealed truth binding on the consciences of the faithful. Many of the older theologians could not have taught it as opposed to Evolution, because they held the six days of creation to be of the ordinary length, and this of course excluded from their minds all idea of a slow process of formation. Perhaps, after all, as far as Faith and ethical results are concerned, this whole question is not of practical consequence.

When we say there is no conflict between Evolution and Faith we speak of course of Theistic Evolution, Atheistic being entirely outside our question. The Evolution system seems to be the more intelligent one. It does not diminish our idea of God's greatness; it increases our idea of His Power. This is clear, because the theory supposes that God made a world with all the germs for Evolution contained in it. The last sentence of Charles Darwin's work, the "Origin of Species," is worth reproducing in this connection. "There is grandeur," he writes, "in this view of life with its several powers, having been originally breathed by the Creator into a few forms or into one ; and that, while this planet has gone cycling on according to the fixed law of gravity, from so simple a beginning endless forms most beautiful and most wonderful have been and are being evolved." Indeed, the process of Evolution, as we understand it in its christianized form, seems to be impossible unless the existence of God be granted. Evolution began in time or it is eternal. If it began in time, how did it originate? We may say, motion caused it. Without motion an egg does not become a bird, a chrysalis does not develop into a butterfly, a leaf does not tremble, an apple does not fall, and so of all the rest. But whence that motion? Now, motion can not produce it, no more than non-existence can produce existence. It must have some cause outside itself, and that cause or force we call God. Nor can it be said that Evolution is eternal. We all know that the world has gone on progressing and has attained a certain limited perfection. Yet this perfection is so curtailed that it leaves much to be desired. If Evolution were eternal it would follow that eternity was not long enough ; in other words, that a time greater than eternity were necessary to bring about a certain finite and qualified perfection.

When the dust and smoke of this great intellectual battle will have cleared away, it may be found that nature leads up to nature's God, that the formation of Eve from Adam's rib is not necessarily destructive of the Evolution theory, but may be accepted as a figure of speech—a way of insisting on the intimacy of the marriage tie—that, as Aristotle's philosophy was not in deadly antagonism to Christianity, and Genesis and Geology not irreconcilable, so, time may show Faith and Evolution to be in accord, the one assisting or at least not opposing the other. The day is not far distant when, as a certain well-known writer remarks, were the first chapter of Genesis some newly-discovered remnant of Arabic literature, or hieroglyphic just deciphered from some Egyptian monument, it would be hailed as a remarkable anticipation of some of the chief events of modern science.

CHAPTER VIII.

THE CHURCH AND THE BIBLE.

IT is strange, yet true, that modern scientific research brings the Bible more and more into prominence every day. The many subjects which are said to be in opposition to its teaching—questions of geology, of astronomy, of history, of biology, etc.,—help to cause this result. We may remark in passing, that truth, from whatever source it comes, can not contradict truth; and therefore real science and real revelation, whether written or unwritten, can not be in opposition. God is the author of all truth. Some truths belong to a higher plane, some to a lower. The verities of each plane or order may run in parallel directions, but they do not and can not oppose each other.

It is too late in the day to tell us we are not allowed to read the Bible. If the very young and the very illiterate at any time in the history of the Church made an unworthy use of certain parts of the sacred book, so as to necessitate a temporary withdrawal of it from them, this must not be construed into a prohibition to Catholics to read the word of God. The Church has ever been the guardian of the Bible. She guarded it for, and gave it to, the laity as well as the clergy. Even in that much-abused medieval period, sermons and other writings contained more scriptural quotations and allusions than similar productions of the present day. The Bible was written originally in the oriental languages— Hebrew, Chaldaic, Greek. From the Apostolic age, we find translations, now of one book of Scripture, again of another, made into Latin, then the spoken tongue of all the Western world. The great Vulgate version of the Bible is a work, partly of revision, partly of translation, done by St. Jerome in the fifth century under the highest auspices of the Church, whilst Latin was still a living and wide-spread language. And when it had ceased to be the language of the people, and the Vulgate became unintelligible to them, translations were made into the many tongues which had grown from the parent of all the languages of Western Europe. "In the eighth and ninth centuries," says Hallam, "when the Vulgate had ceased to be generally intelligible, translations were freely made into the vernacular languages." Then the monks often spent a whole life-time in copying and illuminating the Bible. After the invention of printing, their laborious toil became unnecessary, and the publication of various editions of the Bible was one of the first uses to which this noble art was put. The art of printing was invented three-quarters of a century before Luther burned the Pope's bull, and books were spread far and wide throughout Europe. For over a century after the invention of printing the Bible occupied, more than any other work, the printers of the old world. As early as the year 1500 it was printed more than one hundred times, and Luther's quarrel with the Pope had not reached its climax until 1520. Luther's "discovery" of a copy of the Bible in his monastery at Erfurt is not therefore very wonderful; nor is it true to say that the Reformation first gave the Bible to the people in their own language. Besides this multiplicity of copies in the language of the people, we are encouraged to read the Scriptures, sometimes by individual bishops; sometimes by the bishops of a whole country assembled in council; sometimes by the very highest authority in the Church. As a sort of introduction to our English Catholic Bible, we find a letter from Pope Pius V., in which these words occur: "At a time when a vast number of bad books, which grossly attack the Catholic religion, are circulated even among the unlearned, to the great destruction of souls, it was rightly judged that the faithful should be excited to the reading of the holy Scriptures; for those are the most abundant sources, which ought to be left open to every one, to draw from them purity of morals, and of doctrine, to eradicate the errors which are so widely disseminated in these corrupt times." The bishops of the United States, assembled at the Third Plenary Council of Baltimore, recommended the use of the Bible in the following remarkable words: "It can hardly be necessary to remind you, beloved brethren, that the most highly-valued treasure of every family library, and the most frequently and lovingly made use of, should be the holy Scriptures."

The Bible has come to us through the Church. When it is spoken of as being printed in the language of the people, some seem to forget that there are other languages besides English. Twenty-nine different editions, some of them different versions, were printed in German before Luther's Bible. More than forty editions appeared in Italian before the Protestant Bible saw the light in that language. There were versions published in Flemish and in Bohemian; there were versions in the language of France, once the favorite daughter of the Catholic Church; there were versions published in Spain, the home of the Inquisition, whilst Protestantism was yet a thing of the future. The Reformers were not the first to translate it into English; for we have the high authority of Sir Thomas More for saying, that before the days of Wycliff the whole Bible was translated into the English tongue. People are accustomed to think of it as a well-bound volume, taken down from some book-shelf by order of the Almighty, and safely put in their hands. As a matter of fact, it is made up of a great many books, written at different times, and by different persons, as occasion called for them. It was almost a thousand years after Moses had written the first four books of the Old Testament when the various parts were collected together in one volume. The Epistles and Gospels were written to particular churches or to particular persons. About half a century elapsed between the earliest Gospel, that of St. Matthew; and the latest, that of St. John. Then towards the close of the fourth century all the books of the Old Testament and of the New were collected, and the Canon of Scripture was drawn up precisely as it exists at the present day. It is no exaggeration to say that the Catholic Church had been the sole guardian of the Bible for nearly fifteen hundred years. During the Church of the martyrs her children gave up their lives rather than surrender the sacred volume to be desecrated by the Pagan persecutors. When some few, weaker than their fellows, gave up this treasure, they were called "traitors" (givers-up); and to them this vile term was applied for the first time in the world's history. The Church gathered together the different books and preserved them through ages of ignorance and violence; she afterwards multiplied copies of them, and adorned them with all that art and wealth could furnish; she made them the centre of the whole circle of sacred learning; and when music, and poetry, and painting were cultivated, it was for the chanting of psalms, the singing of mysteries of Holy Writ, or the artistic representation of subjects from the Bible.

The Bible may be viewed under a twofold aspect—as a work of history and as an inspired book. As a history it is deserving of credit, such as any other respectable historical treatise. As an inspired book we go farther. The Church has never given an authentic and complete exposition of the nature of inspiration. It is not enough to say that the Scripture is the best human expression of divine wisdom, for the councils of Florence, Trent, and the Vatican, have defined that the books of Scripture have God for their author. A Catholic is free to hold that inspiration consists in a subsequent divine approbation of the book; or that it consists in a certain accompanying assistance, even though it be only of a negative kind, given by Almighty God to the writer. But the most common teaching of our theologians is that the divine assistance given to the writer of the sacred text is of a positive kind; that it is not only concomitant but also antecedent; that it moves the writer to conceive those things which God wishes him to write; that the writer's will reaches to these only; that the divine influence induces the writer to write these things which God wishes. Catholic doctrine does not compel us to hold that every word in the sacred Scripture is inspired; nor does it force us to the belief that minute matters of detail, put in by way of graphic description, form an inspired part of the sacred narrative. It is well to remember that the great object of Scripture inspiration is faith and moral conduct.

The Catholic Church is the witness of the inspiration of the Bible. If we accept it as God's word, and all Christians do, we must receive it on the testimony of the Catholic Church. She is our only witness, but her evidence is sufficient. Christians of all denominations are forced to acknowledge this. A Protestant finds a Bible in the family. The family may have possessed it as an heirloom since the days of John Wesley or Martin Luther. Thus far they received it on mere human testimony—human in the beginning, human in the end, the "traditions of man." Then we ask ourselves, where did the authors of the Reformation get the Bible? and the answer brings us back to the grand old historic Church which bridges over the chasm that lies between the birth of the great Revolt and the dawn of Christianity or the age of the Apostles. Neither the Scripture itself nor ancient documentary evidence is sufficient to beget a moral certainty of its inspiration. If here and there the New Testament bears witness in some measure to the Old, what will bear witness to the former? Its own testimony will not suffice, for if one should give evidence in his own favor, his witness is nothing. We are in complete accord with Carlyle when he says, in all the world there is no such book beside, for the cottage window or the statesman's closet, the poet's instance or the orator's pattern, or the help of man, or the inspiration of a race. We are pleased to find this vitriolic critic say, it is the one book wherein for thousands of years the spirit of man has found light and nourishment, and a response to whatever was deepest in his heart, yet we can not help maintaining that superhuman wisdom and beauty will not prove its inspiration. These are claimed for the Koran as well as for the Bible; and if they be a proof in the one case, they are equally a proof in the other. They corroborate an existing belief, they may give rise to a certain limited probability, they are by no means enough to prove inspiration, as missionaries have found when they put the Bible into unchristian hands. Nor does documentary evidence suffice to prove it for those who set aside the authority of the Church. That authority being set at naught, the documents of the early heresies must have as much weight for the modern Protestant as the evidence which remains from Catholic sources. Yet many of the ancient heretics such as the Gnostics, rejected as uninspired, books which Protestants admit to the Canon of Scripture at the present time. The only proof which carries conviction is the testimony of the Church of which St. Peter was the zealous head, and St. Paul the soul-stirring preacher.

The Church is the official interpreter of Scripture. That interpretation which regards faith and morals belongs exclusively to the Church. Exegetic interpretation is unofficial and may be made by anybody. Light may be thrown on obscure passages and abstruse Scriptural questions by men of learning and research regardless of their creed. The Bible contains many things hard to be understood. The obscure nature of many Scriptural doctrines calls for an official interpreter. The Church is a spiritual commonwealth. It would be a strange community, a society of confusion, if all the members were allowed to interpret its laws and to act on their own interpretation. The very blunders of those who deny an official and infallible interpreter are the proof of the necessity of such an expounder. Mosheim, the Protestant historian, says, if each one should depend on the light of reason to the exclusion of authority, there would be as many religions as there are heads. It is this unofficial system of interpretation which gives so many different sects to Protestantism, and makes Church-of-England people, and Methodists, and Baptists, and the rest, degrade Christianity by preaching conflicting doctrines to the heathens of Asia and Africa. In England alone, there are two hundred and fifty different religious systems, all begotten of unofficial biblical interpretation. They guide themselves by others in important affairs; their lawyer is their guide in legal matters, their physician in what concerns their health, their banker or their man of business in finance, but in the case of their immortal souls they consult no one. All whose opinion is worth having, even Renan and Strauss, admit that revelation is an acknowledged historical fact. There is the same reason for protecting it as for making it. Surely God did not leave to the sport of man's fancy the explanation of the truth He made known to us. In order that it be of any use to mankind, in other words, in order that it be to us a revelation, there must be a power to interpret it of equal authority with the revealed truth itself. Protestantism in every land has given us an object-lesson in this truth. Germany, for example, the cradle of Reformation, has also been its grave. Without an official interpretation of Holy Writ, Protestantism has dwindled into a natural Theism; its doctrines have become nebulous and vague; and, like dreams, are continually changing their outlines.

The members of the one true Church under the Old Law had recourse to the High-Priest and the Sanhedrim; similarly, we Catholics refer our religious differences to the Church for decision. Yet whilst saying this much for Church authority, we do not exclude rational aids in the domain of Scriptural criticism and exegesis. In common with Protestants and Rationalists, we use philological helps, helps derived from the laws of thought, from the scope, context, subject matter, etc.; and we use historical aids springing from circumstances of time, persons, places, and such like, which influence a writer. Whilst we may and do suggest new meanings of phrases to which the Church has not attached any fixed interpretation, yet the learned of every school admit the reasonableness of not interpreting the Scriptures against the unanimous consent of the Fathers. This is no more of a restraint upon our research, than is an undoubted scientific fact on the investigations of the scientist. It is only the Church's official interpretation which binds us as of Faith. Given an authorized interpretation on the one hand, given a certain scientific fact on the other—not a mere theory or an opinion of a certain school—and the ingenuity of all men for all time will not be able to show any conflict between them. St. Augustine's words may not be amiss here: "And if I ever find anything in these documents (Scriptures) which may seem contrary to truth, I shall assume unhesitatingly that either it is a faulty copy, or that the translation has not attained the sense of what was spoken, or that we have not understood it."

The Church is our guide also as to the Canon of Scripture. By the Canon of Scripture we mean the list of those books which the Church holds as inspired.

Believing that the gates of hell can never prevail against the Church, and therefore that she is infallible, the canonicity of Scripture becomes for us an easy question. It follows as a conclusion from the infallible authority of the Church. It was this infallible teaching which guided the faithful before the Scriptures were written and before the Canon of Scripture was drawn up. Scripture itself really rests on tradition, and were it not for the voice of the Church we could never form a moral certainty as to what books we should admit to the Canon of Scripture and what we should exclude. The Fathers of the Church, assembled at the Council of Hippo in 393, at the third Council of Carthage in 397, and at the sixth Council of Carthage in 419 (their decision was subsequently confirmed by the general Councils of Florence and Trent), ought to be very good authority as to what books we should receive as Canonical Scriptures. Their list is our list, and it reminds us of the well-known saying of St. Augustine: "For my part, I should not believe the Gospel, were I not moved thereto by the authority of the Catholic Church."

The Church also teaches us that Scripture is not our full and complete rule of faith. Tradition is required to complete it. No mere rumor, or hearsay, or local belief, constitutes tradition. It is the unwritten word of God, as Scripture is the written word. The doctrine came first from God, was taught by our Saviour and the Apostles, and through them it was passed on to the early Fathers of the Church, is recorded in their writings, and thus it has come down from generation to generation.

Christ left His Church with nothing but tradition to

guide it. St. Paul, in his Second Epistle to the Thessalonians, insists upon its necessity in these words: "Brethren, stand fast and hold the traditions which you have learnt, whether by word or by our epistle" (ii. 14). All Christian denominations say the Apostles' Creed, and it is tradition which has given it to us; all Christian denominations observe Sunday, and it is tradition which has taught us its observance. This does not in any way lessen our reverence for the written word. The Catholic Church honors and loves the Scriptures. By all means, Catholics should read and study the sacred books, and certainly they ought to derive at least as much profit and pleasure from such study as do our separated brethren.

CHAPTER IX.

THE MEANING OF "OUT OF THE CHURCH NO SALVATION."

THE councils of the Church have been convoked mostly because of some attacks made upon her, either in doctrine or discipline. When a person is attacked, naturally enough he is unwilling to yield any uncontested ground to his aggressor. So also with the Church. Under pressure of an onslaught she states her doctrines in a way, true of course, but uncompromising; sometimes using forms for the proper understanding of which an explanation is necessary. The phrase at the head of this chapter is an illustration. We find it in the Fourth General Council of Lateran, held in the year 1215, and called together to protect the Church principally against the errors of the Albigenses who taught the subversion of ecclesiastical authority; the belief in two Creators and two Christs; that the Sacraments are useless ceremonies; that the body does not rise from the dead; and that the soul is a demon confined within the body in punishment of sin. Ecclesiastical history, we are told, is the right eye of dogmatic theology, and studying the phrase, "Out of the Church no Salvation," under the fierce light of historical criticism, we can readily understand why the doctrine of our Church was stated in a form apparently so narrow.

The population of the earth at the present time is estimated to be about 1,437,150,000. Of this number 217,000,000 are Catholics. That all others should be excluded from salvation, is, to say the least of it, a hard saying. The Church of which there is question here, is the Church established by Jesus Christ on earth. We speak not of the Church triumphant in Heaven, nor of the Church suffering in Purgatory, but of the Church militant on earth. The Church established by our Saviour and recognized by the Apostles is a visible body. There are in it bad as well as good. In St. Matthew's Gospel we find it compared to a field in which good seed and weeds are allowed to grow up together until the day of judgment; to a net in which good and bad fish are caught; to a wedding feast where all the guests have not donned the wedding garments; to virgins of whom some are wise, others foolish.

In order to belong to the visible communion of the Church it is necessary to hold its profession of Faith, not to reject the Sacraments or the Holy Sacrifice, and to acknowledge the supreme rulership of the Sovereign Pontiff in spiritual matters. He who pertinaciously rejects an article of faith becomes a heretic; he who refuses to admit the authority of the Pope in spiritual things becomes a schismatic.

The Church may well be compared to a person. We distinguish in each human being a twofold element: the visible or material, called the body; the invisible or immaterial, called the soul. No one denies the animal nature of man's body. The soul—the immaterial element looking out of its prison-house of clay—with its inherent qualities of memory, of free-will, of reason, and of immortality, makes man lord of creation. As man is composed of body and soul, so also is the Church. Theologians most commonly understand the body of the Church to mean the aggregation of her members. The soul of the Church comprises all those gifts which enable her to perform her offices of bringing unbelievers to faith, of converting sinners to saintliness, and of making the just more perfect. Whoso is in the state of sanctifying grace belongs to the soul of the Church. And he who possesses the state of grace enjoys the friendship of God, is heir to the Kingdom of Heaven, and has all the qualifications required for admission to the beatific vision.

It is not a dogma of Faith that all who are outside the visible communion of the Church will be lost. It is of Faith, that for salvation one should belong, at least, to the soul of the Church. Now, a person may be in a state of sanctifying grace, and yet may not belong to the visible pale of the Church. The proximate rule of morality for each one is his conscience. Conscience is the practical judgment of each person, saying something in particular here and now is to be avoided, inasmuch as it is evil; or is to be done, inasmuch as it is good. It is an act of the intellect, not of the will. It regards one's own actions, not the actions of others. It regards actions done here and now, not actions of the past or of the future. It regards acts under this aspect alone, viz., the lawfulness or unlawfulness of them. The principles which regulate conscience are three :

First, it is never lawful to act against conscience.

Second, it is never lawful to act according to conscience unless there is present a certain dictate of the lawfulness of the act. Doubt must therefore be removed by means, direct or indirect, before action is taken.

Third, it is lawful to do that which a certain conscience says is lawful.

With these principles before our minds, it is evident that for each man his own individual conscience is the highest law, and sin is for him an impossibility so long as he conforms his actions to that conscience. On the other hand, to act against one's conscience without committing sin, is a contradiction in terms, and even God Himself could not make such a thing lawful.

When Christ established His Church, He issued a command that all should belong to it. He sent His Apostles to preach the Gospel to every one, to teach all nations, and the universal command to teach, implied a corresponding universal command to learn. But to belong to the *visible* communion of the Church is not necessary in the same sense that air and water are for life; in other words, it is not necessary as a means. The nature of the necessity is the same as that which binds Catholics to abstain from meat on Friday, that is, it is necessary to belong to the visible pale of the Church, because Christ has issued a command to that effect. Amongst the causes which excuse from a law of this kind, invincible ignorance stands out in bold relief. A man may never have heard of the true Church of Christ, or having heard of it, he may have used all due diligence in looking for the true Church without success. In either case he labors under invincible ignorance. That there are many such people in the world theologians of every school, and from many lands, from France, Spain, Italy, Germany, and Ireland, bear ample testimony. When we consider what are the prejudices of early youth, of an erroneous education, the influence of parents and teachers, of public opinion and public law; in a word, when we remember that man is the creature of his environments, the wonder that many are in good faith, laboring under invincible ignorance, comes at once to an end. The true Church is to many, guiltlessly unknown; and, as Balmez well puts it, an unknown law can not be obligatory. There is no actual punishment without actual sin. There is no actual sin without liberty, and there is no liberty without knowledge. God, therefore, does not punish people for being outside the visible communion of the Church through no fault of their own. But suppose a doubt should present itself to the mind of an outsider, he is bound in conscience to search for the truth, and having found, to accept it. A stanza from Cardinal Newman's well-known hymn sums up the theology of this case:

> "Lead, kindly light, amid the encircling gloom
>   Lead thou me on!
> The night is dark, and I am far from home,
>   Lead thou me on!"

God did not create people to be lost. Our conception of the common Father of all, does not imply that He is a cruel or an unjust God. Nor has our doctrine, when properly understood, any elements of cruelty in it. It is taught in the Epistle of St. Paul to Timothy that God gives to all men opportunities of salvation. "For this is good and acceptable in the sight of God our Saviour, who will have all men to be saved and to come to the knowledge of the truth" (I. Tim. ii. 4–6). He gives to all the means, either proximately or remotely, sufficient for salvation; so that if people be damned, they are lost, not because God created them for eternal punishment, but because they did not make use of the means at their disposal for the attainment of salvation.

In reference to the subject under consideration, those who are outside the visible communion of the Church may be divided into three classes, namely, children who die without Baptism, baptized Protestants, and pagans. Punishment in the next world is twofold: the pain of loss and the pain of sense. The former consists in the absence of the beatific vision, or not seeing God; the latter, in the positive suffering inflicted. It is not true to say that our Church teaches as an article of Faith that children who die without Baptism are condemned to any pain of sense. They are excluded from the Kingdom of Heaven, and Catholic doctrine limits itself to this privation. Indeed, it would appear contrary to the bounteous mercy of the All-Wise if personal suffering were inflicted in the next life where there had been no personal sin in this.

The Almighty, in the distribution of His grace, sincerely wishes the salvation of these children. Certain causes prevent the application of baptism—the means or remedy provided by God. As universal Provider, He is not bound to stop by miracle the effect of these causes. From this, however, it by no means follows that unbaptized children will have to endure the pain of sense. As to the loss of the beatific vision, we must remember that eternal happiness is not natural to man. Unbaptized children have not in them the principle of eternal life. The privation of the beatific vision is not to them a harshness. They may not even know that there is such a thing as a beatific vision. It is the teaching of St. Thomas that they enjoy God by a natural knowledge and love. It is the teaching of theologians of the highest authority, that children who die without baptism, so far from being punished by the pain of sense, or even the pain of loss, will enjoy the highest form of natural happiness, higher than any attainable by man on earth. God is just; therefore He will not punish the innocent.

The possibility of salvation for baptized Protestants does not present any serious difficulty. It is not the teaching of the Catholic Church that all Protestants will be lost. They may follow the dictates of conscience, as they are really bound to do. They may be in invincible ignorance of the true Church, in which case all theologians agree that they are not culpable in the eyes of God for not entering it. Invincible ignorance excuses them from the command of belonging to the body of the Church, and if they be in a state of sanctifying grace, they belong to the soul of the Church. It is the teaching of the Church that any one—Jew, or Pagan, or Protestant—may baptize validly. All who are baptized are Christians. In Baptism the virtues of Faith, Hope, and Charity, are infused into the soul. The baptized possess the power of making acts of divine faith, and grievous sin does not destroy that power. All Christians hold the necessity of Faith for salvation. "But without faith it is impossible to please God" (Rom. xi. 6). Human faith is not sufficient; divine faith is necessary. We believe, not on the authority of man as such, but on the authority of God. God may speak to us through man as His prophet, or His messenger, or His ambassador. And here we have to make an important distinction between divine faith and Catholic faith. All Catholic faith is divine, but all divine faith is not Catholic. Divine faith is the sacred deposit contained in the Scriptures and in the traditions of the Church. A truth is not of Catholic faith (even though that truth be contained in the sacred deposit) until it is formally proposed by the Church for our acceptance. Catholic faith is not necessary for all. It is not necessary for those who are in guiltless ignorance of the true Church. Divine faith is sufficient, and divine faith Protestants can have. "To believe," says St. Thomas, "is an act of the intellect assenting to divine truth by command of the will moved by the grace of God." The motive of divine faith is the authority of God revealing a truth. Baptized Protestants may have this motive; they may believe on the authority of God. They may use private judgment to find out the truth, but God's truth and God's will they make supreme, and would not willingly make them secondary to their own views. Hence we conclude that there is a possibility of salvation for baptized Protestants.

But what of the possibility of salvation for pagans? Is there no hope for them? We shall see. The teaching of our theologians is summed up in the axiom: "*Facienti quod in se est, Deus non denegat gratiam*"—"To him who does what he can, God will not deny grace." They are bound to obey the law of nature; God gives them grace for its observance. If this divine gift be well used, God will be still more generous, until finally the light of faith shines in the intellect of the unbeliever. God, by reason of His will to save all, most certainly gives grace to every one who does not put obstacles in the way. Even those who never heard of God or Christ, or Christianity, or the Church, can come to the knowledge of a Supreme Being from the light of reason alone. "But that which is known of God is manifest in them. For God has manifested it to them. For the invisible things of Him, from the creation of the world, are clearly seen, being understood by the things that are made; His eternal power also and His divinity; so that they are inexcusable" (Romans i. 19, 20). The voice of conscience also tells them of a responsibility to a Higher Power. The "still small voice" tells them that certain things are bad, and they know that the Supreme Being is a rewarder of the good things and a punisher of the bad. There is no such thing as a Pagan pure and simple. There was given to Adam a primitive revelation, and howsoever obscured this may have become, yet it is still the heritage of all mankind. It is worth while noting in this connection the teaching of the great Spanish theologian, Lugo, regarding Jews and Mohammedans. He says, they can have supernatural faith in God, and other divine truths propounded in Holy Scripture, which they receive from tradition, and having that faith, can therefore be justified and saved. The teaching of St. Thomas regarding the guileless heathen has almost become commonplace from quotation. He writes: "God would give an interior revelation of the truths necessary to believe, or send him a preacher of the faith as He sent Peter to Cornelius."

If all this be true, if people can be saved without being members of the visible communion of the Church, what is the advantage of being a Catholic? It must be remembered that no one can lose the true Faith, except through his own fault; it must be borne in mind, that when a doubt presents itself to one who is outside the visible pale of the Church, he is bound to investigate; it must not be forgotten, that when one knows the true Church he is bound to join it. God's words are committed to the guardianship of the true Church. Those who do not belong to the body of the Church have not the benefits of the Sacraments. They lose the gifts given to man through these channels of grace. Marvelous as are the secret workings of nature, still more wonderful are the secret effects of divine grace in the soul. The seven Sacraments correspond with the seven stages in man's life. Each Sacrament gives a grace common to all the others, and also a grace peculiar to itself, having for its object the end for which the Sacrament was instituted. There are many other spiritual aids given to those who belong to the visible communion of the Church. It is very difficult for those who have not the graces given through the Sacraments, especially the Sacraments of Penance and Holy Eucharist, to lead a life without falling into one grievous sin at least. Then the only means of salvation is by perfect contrition. And, after having led a careless life, it is not an easy matter to make an act of perfect love of God. The sum of our teaching is this: There is a *possibility* of salvation for all; there is a comparative *facility* of salvation for those who belong to the visible communion of the Church. Thus we see how beautifully the mercy and justice of God are made to harmonize; we see how Christianity loses none of its joyousness by a teaching needlessly severe; we learn a doctrine calculated not to break men's hearts, but to melt them to divine love, and to an acknowledgment of the Fatherhood of God.

CHAPTER X.

INDULGENCES.

MORE than half a century ago a writer in a British review called attention to the deplorable ignorance among non-Catholics concerning Indulgences, an ignorance reaching from Southey, the poet-laureate of that day, down to the dullest unbeliever in all England. We may add that even at the present time there is not a doctrine of the Church about which there is more misunderstanding, as is evident from the pulpit utterances, and books, even histories, of our separated brethren.

Words sometimes change their meaning with lapse of time. Thus, the word "prevent," at one time meant to go before, now it means to stop, to hinder ; "tempt," meant to try, to prove, now it means to solicit to evil; "offend," to cause to err, now means to displease, or to injure. In an old English version of the New Testament St. Paul is called the *villain* of Jesus Christ. The epithet will not astonish us, if we remember that the word "villain" then meant servant. Thus, also, has the word "indulgence" changed its meaning. Formerly it meant *favor, remission,* or *forgiveness*; now it is sometimes taken in the sense of unlawful gratification. This latter meaning easily suggested the idea that an indulgence is a license to commit sin. We shall see that so far from being a liberty to sin, it is an incentive to virtue.

In the theological sense, the word "indulgence" implies an act of clemency on the part of the Church. An Indulgence is a remission of the punishment which is still due to sin after the guilt, and therefore the eternal punishment is forgiven, this remission being valid in the court of conscience and before God, and being made by the application of the treasure of the Church on the part of a lawful superior. Whatever may be said on the dark question of the origin of evil, we are certain that sin exists; that some sins do not exclude from the kingdom of Heaven, as those committed by him who falls several times a day and yet is a just man; that other sins will shut us out for ever from God, such as those mentioned in the partial list drawn up by St. Paul: "Know you not that the unjust shall not possess the kingdom of God? Do not err. Neither fornicators, nor idolaters, nor adulterers, nor the effeminate, nor liars with mankind, nor thieves, nor covetors, nor drunkards, nor railers, nor extortioners, shall possess the kingdom of God" (I. Cor. vi. 9, 10).

All Catholic theologians agree in distinguishing between the guilt or offense of sin, and its punishment. The offense is the injury done to God; the punishment is the chastisement that God has a right to inflict. They distinguish the punishment which is eternal, and the punishment which is merely temporal. The offense or guilt of sin, and its eternal punishment, are chiefly forgiven by the Sacraments of Baptism and Penance, and not by an Indulgence. An act of perfect love of God will also reconcile the sinner with the Eternal Father. Venial sin may of course be blotted out by Sacramental absolution, but forgiveness of it may also be obtained by various other acts of piety, such as hearing Mass, saying the Lord's Prayer, using piously any object blessed by the Church. Sometimes one's love of God may be so all-consuming that it leaves no place even for temporal punishment. Usually the temporal punishment remains. We have many Scriptural examples of this. In the twelfth chapter of the Book of Numbers we are told that Mary, the sister of Moses, committed sin by murmuring against him. She repented, yet a temporal punishment of leprosy, and of a seven days' separation from her people, was imposed upon her. Adam repented of his sin, yet the Lord told him he should eat with labor and toil for the rest of his days. Moses sinned by want of confidence in God. He was a sincere penitent and was therefore forgiven. God, however, would not allow him to enter the promised land. What is this but a temporal punishment? Aaron committed the same sin and died in Mt. Hor, instead of in the Land of Promise. Perhaps the most conspicuous example of our doctrine of temporal punishment is to be found in the case of David. "And David said to Nathan: I have sinned against the Lord. And Nathan said to David: The Lord also hath taken away thy sin; thou shalt not die. Nevertheless, because thou hast given occasion to the enemies of the Lord to blaspheme, for this thing, the child that is born to thee shall surely die" (II. Kings xii. 13, 14).

St. Augustine taught the existence of temporal punishment in the words: "O Lord, Thou dost not leave unpunished the sins of even those to whom Thou grantest pardon" (Comment on Ps. 50, n. ii.).

The doctrine of Indulgences rests upon two others—the Communion of Saints, and the existence of a spiritual treasury in the Church. The members of God's Church are bound together by a common bond. The Communion of Saints gives them a community of spiritual goods in the Church. By virtue of this community of spiritual interests the faithful have power mutually to assist each other. By virtue of the Communion of Saints, the good that is done by individuals in the Christian commonwealth promotes in some measure the good of all, just as citizens who possess civic virtue and honest enterprise advance the interests of the whole community. All the good acts of the just have a twofold value, namely, that of merit and that of satisfaction. One merits for himself; but the satisfaction, or atonement, or compensation, or payment of a debt, or whatever else we choose to call it, may be applied to another. There is nothing objectionable, and there is much to be admired in a man paying the debts of his needy friends. The satisfaction made to God is merely a payment from the rich spiritual treasury of the Church, due to the Almighty by reason of the temporal punishment due to sin. Christ's atonement for sin was so great "that where sin abounded, grace has superabounded" (Rom. v. 20). The satisfaction made by Him was either infinite, or practically the same as infinite. Suppose the planets were inhabited, suppose millions of worlds were created and as thickly peopled as China is to-day, the satisfaction of Christ to His Father would be enough and more than enough for all. A very small act on the part of Christ would have been enough to redeem the world, but He offered His whole being in sacrifice. As this sacrifice can not be unprofitable it goes to make up the treasury of the Church. God's mother had no sin, and therefore no temporal punishment for which to satisfy. Her satisfaction, the result of a life of good works, goes to swell the spiritual treasury of the Church. Then there are the satisfactory works of the saints. Many of them, doubtless, offered satisfaction far beyond any due for their sins. All this superabundance is not forgotten by God. As the good works of the saints derive their value from Christ, they do not decrease His honor, but show forth His Glory. "There is no need," writes Cardinal Bellarmine, "to unite the sufferings of the saints with those of our Divine Lord, as, if the latter were not sufficient in themselves, they are joined to these honors, because it is fitting that their sufferings should not be unprofitable before God, particularly since such a course, besides tending in a high degree to glorify the Redeemer from Whom these holy ones derive all their blessings, redounds very much to the honor of the saints themselves" (De Indul. lib. 1, chap. 7).

The power of granting Indulgences belongs to the Pope for the whole Church, and to the bishops for their respective dioceses. A plenary Indulgence is the remission of all the temporal punishment of which one is worthy in the eyes of God. A plenary Indulgence is rarely gained to its fullest extent, and we can not know when it is. In order to understand the meaning of a partial Indulgence, we must recall to mind the public penances which were wont to be imposed in the early days of the Church. They were very severe, sometimes consisting of a fast on bread and water for a whole lifetime, or for a long term of years. A partial Indulgence is the remission of as much of the temporal punishment as would have been remitted by the performance of canonical penance for a corresponding length of time.

Thus when an Indulgence of forty days or forty years is granted, it means that there is forgiven as much of the temporal punishment as would have been blotted out by forty days or forty years of canonical penance. We do not, and we can not, know the full extent to which Indulgences cancel temporal punishment with God. That depends on the dispositions of the persons and on the amount of debt due to the Almighty. Some Indulgences are granted without limit as to time; some for a specified time. The former are called perpetual; the latter, temporary. Sometimes Indulgences may be gained only in a particular place, and are called local; sometimes they are granted immediately and directly to persons, for instance, to an order or confraternity, and are called personal; sometimes they are attached to things, such as crucifixes, medals, etc., and are called real.

Two things, and only two, are of Catholic Faith regarding Indulgences. These are: first, the Church has power to grant them; second, their use is eminently salutary to a Christian people. Other things may be almost articles of Faith, such as, the temporal punishment due to sin is blotted out by Indulgences; some Indulgences may be applied to the souls in Purgatory; there is in the Church a spiritual treasury made up of the satisfactions of Christ and the saints; but only the two points mentioned are we bound to accept as articles of our Faith.

That the Church has power to grant Indulgences we know from several sources. Christ addressed St. Peter in these words: "I will give to thee the keys of the kingdom of heaven; and whatsoever thou shalt bind upon earth, it shall be bound also in heaven; and whatsoever thou shalt loose on earth, it shall be loosed in heaven" (Matt. xvi. 17). In similar language He conveyed the same meaning to all the Apostles (xviii. 18). The words must be taken in their broadest signification, as there is question of conferring a favor. To the power granted there is no limit assigned in the text, nor in the context, nor in any other part of the Sacred Scripture, and the practice of the Church from the days of the Apostles has been to grant Indulgences. The words of the text show, that power has been given to remove every obstacle which prevents one from entering heaven. Temporal punishment is an obstacle; therefore power is given to remove it. The same conclusion follows from the usage of speech. The metaphor of the keys shows it. When we say a man has the keys of any place, the clear meaning is that he can open the doors and get us admission to it.

The power of granting Indulgences was exercised in the Church of Apostolic times. Paul granted an Indulgence to the criminal Corinthian. This man had been condemned to a severe medicinal punishment. He repented, and Paul freed him from the penalty previously imposed. "To him that is such a one, this rebuke is sufficient, which is given by many. So that contrariwise you should rather pardon and comfort him, lest, perhaps, such a one be swallowed up with overmuch sorrow. * * * * And to whom you have pardoned anything, I also. For, what I have pardoned, if I have pardoned anything, for your sakes I have done it, in the person of Christ" (II. Cor. ii. 6–10). The teaching that the Church has power to grant Indulgences is handed down to us in a manner clear, constant, uninterrupted, and universal, from the days of the

Apostles. History tells us of barbarous persecutions of the early Christians. The first three centuries of the Church's existence are known as the period of the Church of the martyrs. The tortures were so savagely severe that we must not be surprised if some of the Christians apostatized, or pretended to have done so. Many of them were afterwards truly penitent. They frequently brought letters of recommendation from those who were about to be martyred. On the strength of these letters the bishops applied to the penitents the superabundant satisfactions of the martyrs and lessened the penance which they should otherwise undergo. In the third century St. Cyprian wrote these words: "Since I find that it will not yet be in my power to come amongst you * * * * * I think that the case of our brethren ought to be met, so that they who have received tickets from the martyrs and who have been helped by their privilege from God * * * * may go before the Lord with that peace which the martyrs, by their letters unto us, have desired might be granted." This manner of granting Indulgences ended with the persecutions. But the Councils of the Church, her saints and her representative men, such as Basil the Great in the fourth century, and Leo the Great in the sixth, make frequent reference to the fact that the bishops of this period continuously granted Indulgences to deserving penitents. In the ninth century began the custom of changing the canonical penances into something less severe; to the saying of psalms, the giving of alms, etc. In 1095, Pope Urban the Second granted an Indulgence to all who, for religious reasons, should join the crusade against the Saracens for the recovery of the Holy Land and should die in God's friendship whilst engaged in this work. And so through all the ages we can trace the uniform teaching of the Church on Indulgences, from the Leo of our time, the patron of all that is beautiful and good, to the patron of art and of letters, Leo the Tenth, who gave Luther the pretext for revolt. And from this Leo we trace our doctrine through the chivalrous days of the crusades, backward and yet further back till we come to the time when Paul rebuked and yet obeyed Peter.

There is really nothing wonderful in the fact that the Church has power to grant Indulgences. An Indulgence is a favor. The ruler of every community or society, be it ever so small, grants favors at times. The head of a family, the mayor of a city, the governor of a state, the ruler of a nation, all grant favors or Indulgences of a kind other than spiritual. What wonder then if the chief of a spiritual kingdom should grant spiritual Indulgences? Let us take an example. A criminal is sentenced to a life-long imprisonment. By his exemplary conduct he attracts the attention of the officials, until finally the mind of the governor or of the president is directed to the case. The ruler may grant remission of the whole punishment, or he may give a punishment vastly lighter. This latter is what the Church does in her spiritual kingdom.

In order to gain an Indulgence we must have an intention of doing so. Whatever may be said as to the nature of that intention, it is certain that if one makes up his mind in the morning to gain all the Indulgences of the day, this intention perseveres. A second condition is, the faithful performance as to time, place, and manner, of the works prescribed. The third chief condition is the state of grace, at least when the last prescribed work is performed. This is reasonable. An Indulgence is a favor, and we can not expect a favor from him with whom we are at enmity. No Indulgence can be obtained for an unforgiven sin. No matter how venial or small a sin may be, it cannot be forgiven by an Indulgence. Let it be written in letters of gold; that to gain an Indulgence one must be free from grave sin and therefore sincerely desirous of leading a good life.

With a strange persistency some writers tell us Leo the Tenth, in Luther's time, and the Church at other times, sold Indulgences. In fact, the Council of Trent wishes that spiritual graces should be given not only gratuitously, but in such a way as to exclude altogether the imputation of temporal motives. Leo the Tenth was anxious to complete the Church of St. Peter, commenced by Julius the Second. Among the conditions laid down for gaining some Indulgences, an alms, to be devoted to some good purpose, is sometimes asked. Pope Leo intended the alms of the faithful, given on the occasion of the Indulgence granted by him, to go towards the building of that magnificent Church, which is an honor to Christendom. This is a very different thing from selling an Indulgence. A few years ago Leo the Thirteenth granted the Indulgence of the Jubilee, and one of the conditions was that an alms proportionate to the means of each person be given. One of the objects towards which these alms went, was the maintenance of the schools of the East. All agree that this was praiseworthy. All should agree that the similar action of Leo the Tenth was equally praiseworthy. It can not be shown, and it is not true, that Leo the Tenth, or any of his predecessors, or any of his successors, authorized, or encouraged, or permitted the sale of Indulgences. The Church must not be held responsible for the action of officious and irresponsible individuals. Abuses sprang up, but were quickly denounced. The Church denounced them in the Council of Lateran held under Innocent the Third, in the Council of Lyons under Innocent the Fourth, and that before the days of the Reformers. The mind of the Church in condemnation of all such abuses is made known by the Council of Trent in these words: "Wishing to correct and amend the abuses which have crept into them, and on the occasion of which this signal name of Indulgences is blasphemed by heretics, the holy Synod enjoins in general, by the present decree, that all wicked traffic for obtaining them, which has been the fruitful source of many abuses among Christian people, should be wholly abolished."

Nor must it be forgotten that some Indulgences may be applied to the souls in Purgatory. Some Indulgences are granted as applicable to these poor souls. The Church has no direct jurisdiction over them. But the faithful may offer satisfaction to God with a prayer that He may accept it in behalf of the occupants of Purgatory.

Indulgences have many advantages. They blot out temporal punishment, not merely in the eyes of the Church, but before God. This follows as a corollary from the power of granting them. If by virtue of that power every obstacle to the kingdom of Heaven can be removed, it is clear, temporal punishment is really remitted before God. They do not discountenance acts of penance and mortification. Usually, Sacramental Penance is not enough to cover our liabilities to God.

Those are the best children of the Church who avail themselves of Indulgences. Besides being a substitute for the old canonical penance and blotting out temporary punishment, Indulgences are a corrective and a preventive; they encourage to repentance; they induce people to do good works; they promote frequent recourse to the Sacraments of Penance and the Eucharist.

CHAPTER XI.

THEOLOGY OF THE DEVOTION TO THE SACRED HEART.

MAY is the month of the Virgin Mother; June, of devotion to the Sacred Heart of her divine Son. Doctrine leads to devotion. Theology, as a science, may exist without religion, but religion can not hold its ground without theology. The consideration now of this holy subject, now of that, calls forth attention and piety. Christ's desire to be loved by men is ardent and intense. Deeper and more boundless than the ocean is the love of the Sacred Heart of Jesus for mankind.

In the history of His Passion, as recorded in the sacred narrative, we read: "But one of his soldiers with a spear opened his side, and immediately there came out blood and water" (John xix. 38). There is no stronger testimony of the actuality of Christ's death, than this issue of blood and water from His side; and it would appear that the proximate cause was rupture of the heart, the more remote being crucifixion. We have the highest medical authority for saying that natural emotions, when in overwhelming excess, sometimes produce rupture of the heart. And, as Sir James Simpson points out, "if ever a human heart was riven by the mere amount of mental agony that was endured, it would surely be that of our Redeemer." When blood is allowed to stand for some time, it separates itself into the parts of which it is composed. The principal elements of human blood are a colorless liquid substance like water, and certain minute particles (corpuscles) mostly red, which give color to the blood.

Assuming that Christ died of a broken heart, blood flowed into the capsule or membraneous sac which surrounds it. Here being allowed to stand for some time, it resolved itself into the elements just mentioned, so that when the soldier pierced our Lord's side there flowed forth two substances: one resembling water, the other, blood. Thus we can explain, in a satisfactory and scientific manner, the flow from the side of Christ as mentioned by the Evangelist.

Now, it is this Sacred Heart, a Heart literally broken on the cross for love of mankind, that we are asked to honor in a special manner during the month of June. The object, therefore, of our veneration or cultus is the Sacred Heart of Jesus; in other words, the Heart of the Incarnate Word. It is the Heart of the God-man, hence a divine and adorable Heart. We adore it as the Heart of the Person of the Word to which it is inseparably united. This is the visible or corporal object; our veneration has also a spiritual one. The devotion to the Five Wounds, for example, has for its visible object the Sacred Wounds themselves, and for its spiritual object, the suffering of the Man-God revealed through them. Similarly the spiritual object of devotion to the Sacred Heart is the limitless love of Jesus for mankind as made known through it.

The end proposed in venerating the Sacred Heart, is to gain a return of love for Christ's boundless affection, and to make up in some way for the coldness and ingratitude of the greater part of mankind.

The highest form of worship is due to it. Hence we venerate the Sacred Heart with a veneration different from and greater than that which we give to the Virgin Mary. It is the same as that due to the Father, the same as that due to the Holy Ghost, the same as that due to the Blessed Trinity.

The motives of our veneration to the Sacred Heart are manifold. Making use of the popular idea that the heart is the seat of love, Christ proposes to us His Sacred Heart as the seat of His pious affections. These He wishes us to accept and imitate, for He says: "Learn of me, because I am meek and humble of heart" (Matt. xi. 29). By the unanimous consent of men, and the universal usage of speech, consecrated by Scriptural custom, the heart is the symbol of love; therefore the Heart of Jesus is the symbol of His burning love and ardent charity by which He endured so much to redeem us, and instituted the Sacrament of His love for us. A third motive is, as the Sacred Heart is the symbol of Christ's love for us, it reminds us of His sufferings and death, and brings a certain pressure upon us to return affection for the countless benefits for which we are indebted to Him.

As there are two natures, two wills, two intelligences in Christ, so in a certain sense we may say there are two hearts. In the Book of Genesis we read that when the Lord beheld the wickedness of man, He was touched with sorrow of heart. David is spoken of as a man after God's own heart. Thus is the language of man used by the inspired writer, and the sanctity and love of God spoken of under the symbol of the heart. This is the eternal heart of God. The Heart of Jesus is a Heart of flesh, a Heart formed from

Mary Immaculate, a symbol, if you will, for it best symbolizes the love of Jesus for humanity; but it is much more than this, it is also a reality.

In the schools of Theology, where doctrine is generally stated in conservative form, the teaching on the present subject is stated in these words: the veneration of the Sacred Heart, as approved by the Holy See and practised in the Catholic Church, is pious and free from every stain of superstition. It is not proposed as an article of Catholic Faith; it is put forward as a doctrine which is certain, which none but the rash will reject, which can not be set aside without danger of heresy, and therefore without mortal sin.

The foundation of all doctrines which depend on the Incarnation is to be sought in the union of the Divine Word with human nature. The principle on which our adoration of the Sacred Heart rests, is as old as the belief in the hypostatic union. And even if it be said that devotion to the Sacred Heart actually began with the Blessed Margaret Mary Alacoque in the latter part of the seventeenth century, it must be remembered that though the doctrine of the Church does not change, yet, from time to time, she introduces new forms of devotion.

Although there are two natures, two wills, and two intelligences in Jesus Christ, yet there is in Him but one person, and that is the Divine. In his letter to the Philippians, St. Paul writes: " For let this mind be in you, which was also in Christ Jesus; Who, being in the form of God, thought it not robbery to be equal with God: But emptied himself, taking the form of a servant, being made in the likeness of men, and in habit found as a man. He humbled himself, becoming obedient even unto death : even to the death of the cross. For which cause God also hath exalted him, and hath given him a name which is above all names : That in the name of Jesus every knee should bow, of those that are in heaven, on earth, or under the earth" (ii. 5-10). In the first part of this extract the actions of the Divine nature in Jesus are attributed to one person, and that the Divine one. In the second part, the actions of Christ's human nature are attributed to the same Divine person. Hence human nature in Christ has no personality, so that all the acts of the Man, Christ, can be said to be done by God. The humanity of Christ never had personality, and therefore never lost it. It was united to the Divine personality from the first instant of conception. By virtue of this union, the face which men saw nearly nineteen hundred years ago, when Christ was on earth, was the face of God; and the words of consolation addressed to the penitent Magdalene, were the words of God ; and the feet that poor Mary kissed in her passionate repentance were the feet of God; and the brow that was bedecked with a crown of thorns was the brow of God ; and the hands and the feet that were pierced with the nails on that ugly hill were the hands and the feet of God ; and the side that was opened by the spear of the soldier was the side of God ; and the blood that was shed for the redemption of the human race was the blood of God ; and the heart which was broken on the cross was the heart of God; because the whole humanity which was assumed by the Second Person of the Blessed Trinity was the humanity of God. We can now understand why supreme adoration is due to the Sacred Heart of Jesus. The reason is, because the Sacred Heart of Jesus is the

Sacred Heart of God. As such it calls for that highest homage which we give to God alone. By virtue of the hypostatic union, the Second Person of the adorable Trinity is united to the humanity of Christ and to every part of that humanity, such as the human soul is united to the body and to every part of that body. Nor can the humanity of Christ be separated from His Divinity. If it were separated it would no longer be the humanity of Christ, but something else. Neither can the Sacred Heart be separated from the Divinity, and if it were separated, it would cease to be the Sacred Heart of Jesus.

There are reasons for directing our veneration to the Sacred Heart. The Incarnate Word presents Himself to be adored in His human nature. The Sacred Heart of Jesus—a Heart holy with the sanctity of the Word, as well as with the sacredness of a noble soul—is the noblest part of the Divine humanity, and as such is worthy of special reverence. Although when venerating the Sacred Heart we venerate the Divine personality, yet the Heart of Jesus is singled out, because it is the Heart of God, and because it symbolizes Christ's love for our race. It is the object of our love ; it is the symbol of His.

The testimony of the Fathers of the early Church must be of interest to us on this question, especially as devotion to the Sacred Heart did not reach its full development until the latter part of the seventeenth century. St. Augustine, the great African saint, the champion of pure Christianity in his time, writes : " O Heart, fountain of living waters, let me drink and rejoice; Longinus has opened for me the side of Jesus." St. Bonaventura also says : " In the side of Jesus I wish to rest, there I will speak to His Heart, and obtain from

Him what I wish." The key to understand the veneration of the Sacred Heart is, that in Christ there is one Divine Person, and there are two natures—the human and the divine. "This," as the Fathers of the Council of Chalcedon said, "is the doctrine of our forefathers."

Though absorbed in the glory of the divinity, the Sacred Heart still preserves its character of humanity. It is therefore a Heart possessing human sympathy, as was shown at the gates of Naim and at the tomb of Lazarus. It longs to kindle on earth the fire of Divine love, to move men to a larger understanding and to a more mutual brotherhood. Its sympathy reaches to the poor outcast, for Christ came to bring back sinners to His Father. It is a Heart full of gratitude, for not even a sup of cold water is given in the name of Jesus without a recognition and a reward from that grateful Heart. Imitation is the sincerest tribute. It is impossible to estimate how much better the world would be if the adoration, which our theology teaches us is due to the Sacred Heart, were given in the form of imitation—by copying its gentleness, its patience, its sympathy, its desire of universal brotherhood.

CHAPTER XII.

VENERATION OF THE BLESSED VIRGIN.

BY veneration we acknowledge the superior excellence of another, and show our respect because of it. The motive of all veneration is excellence. As there are various species of the latter, so does veneration vary accordingly. Excellence or worth, may be infinite and eternal, as it is in God and in Him alone. It may be merely created, but supernatural, such as the saints possess; or there may be question of natural worth, as genius, learning, bravery, and the like. If the worth be infinite and eternal, then the highest form of cult is due. This is given to God and to Him alone. If we speak of created but supernatural worth, then the veneration of saints has a place. When the excellence is no more than natural and created greatness, such as sublime poets, or soul-stirring orators, or brave soldiers can claim, then we give civil or social veneration. Supernatural and natural greatness belong to different, but not conflicting orders; the one occupying a high plane, the other a lower. The former leads to life eternal; the latter, whilst good and to be admired, has no positive relationship to the object of life.

Yet another distinction. We claim for the Virgin an excellence beyond all other created beings, except the human soul of Jesus. On account of this a higher form of veneration is due to her than to the other saints. Let it, however, be distinctly understood that it is very different from the honor we give to God. The motive is different. In the one case it is excellence infinite and eternal; in the other it is supernatural and supereminent, but withal, created greatness. The species of veneration is different in kind; it differs only in degree from that given to the other saints. God alone we adore with the supremest form of worship. To the Almighty alone we are permitted to offer the Holy Sacrifice, for it is the highest act of adoration. Not to the saints, nor to the Virgin Mary can the Mass be offered, but we may commemorate their memory and have the Holy Sacrifice offered in their honor, that they who have gone before us may intercede for us before God's throne. To give to the Blessed Virgin the worship which belongs to the Almighty is to be guilty of idolatry —a most grievous sin. The difference between the Creator and the created, however gifted and privileged the latter may be, must ever remain infinite; and, therefore, there must ever be an essential difference between the adoration of God and the veneration of Mary.

The veneration of the saints, and therefore of the Blessed Virgin, is lawful and useful. This is our thesis and is Catholic doctrine. The following are our proofs: Civic honors may lawfully and laudably be given to heroes. Reason and Scripture prove it. In all times there has been a unanimity of consent regarding it; so much so, that those who refuse to do honor to men who have deserved well of the community are justly considered malevolent. The memory of our own Washington is honored in many ways. His birthday is kept as a national holiday, pilgrimages are made to his last resting-place on the banks of the Potomac, mementoes and relics are sought with the greatest eagerness, monuments proclaim his deeds of bravery. Cicero (De Natura Deorum) says: "Whoso excels has a claim to just veneration." God's word confirms this popular idea: "Render therefore to all men their dues * * * * to whom *honor*, *honor*" (Rom. xiii. 7). Further evidence is given in the Epistle of St. Paul to Timothy: "Let the priests that rule well be esteemed worthy of a double *honor*, especially they who labor in the word and doctrine" (v. 17). The only reason that is or can be assigned for such honor, is that its recipients excel in some way. If superiority in some walk in life entitles a man to civic honor, surely on the same principle, heroic sanctity should entitle him to religious veneration.

God honors the saints and angels. The Old Law was promulgated directly by them, or by Almighty God, with the angels as assistant ministers. "Who have received the law by the disposition of the angels" (Acts vii. 53). Whichever interpretation we give these words, they are proof of an honor conferred by God. Christ will come with His angels and judge the world, and thus will pay them a high tribute of respect. The parts of the Scripture which tell us the glory and bliss of the saints in Heaven are so much evidence that God honors them. Universal usage explains the meaning of all this. When a ruler honors a subject it is clear he means others likewise to respect him; so, when God honors the saints and makes that known to us through the Sacred Scriptures, we reasonably infer that He wishes us also to venerate them. A confirmation of this is found in the Canticle of the Blessed

Virgin, the Magnificat. There we are told that God made Mary great, and on this account, all generations shall call her blessed, in other words, shall honor her.

The saints and angels pray for us, guard us, love us, and are interested in our salvation. "And the smoke of the incense of the prayers of the saints ascends up before God from the hand of the angel" (Apoc. viii. 4). Such an offering of the prayers of the faithful is really intercession for us. That they guard us Christ teaches in His sermon on humility : "See that you despise not one of these little ones, for I say to you that their angels in Heaven always see the face of My Father, Who is in Heaven" (Matt. xviii. 10). Their love for and interest in us is proven from the joy existing in Heaven before the angels of God for one repentant sinner. That they are so well disposed towards us as to watch over us during life, and to rejoice at our triumph over sin, and to move in our favor the hand of Him Who moves the universe, plainly shows them to be worthy of veneration. Every reason that appeals to us in favor of venerating the saints has a greater force when there is question of honoring Mary—the Queen of all saints. And if we give her a veneration greater than that which is given to the other saints, it is because she excels them. Her Immaculate Conception, her Virginity, and her Motherhood of God, secure a niche in the fane of sanctity higher and more conspicuous than what is due to the other saints. Her privilege of Immaculateness, her gift of avoiding all, even venial faults, her long life of merit, her having united a "mother's love with maiden purity," prepare us to hear her blessedness so frequently mentioned in the Gospel. When we read the salute of Gabriel, "Hail, full of Grace," and find old age paying tribute to her as in the Elizabethan address, "Blessed art thou among women;" and learn that she is the subject of saintly panegyric clearly marking out her position beyond the other saints; we realize the grand fitness of the teaching that her honor should be greater than theirs. All our veneration condensed would not equal even one of the countless acts of honor done by Jesus to Mary when He went down to Nazareth and "was subject to them."

St. Thomas of Aquin says, her sanctity is everything but infinite, and Suarez, the great Spanish theologian whose holiness equaled his learning, teaches that Mary possessed more sanctity than all the other saints and angels together. St. Ephraim, the brightest ornament of the Oriental Church in the fourth century, uses the following language in reference to Mary—words particularly striking in that they are the very terms which the Church of the present day makes use of in order to express the supereminent sanctity of the Mother of God. "We fly to thy patronage, holy Mother of God; protect and guard us under the wings of thy mercy and kindness. Most merciful God, through the intercession of the Blessed Virgin Mary, and of all the angels and saints, show pity to thy creatures. In thee, Patroness and Mediatrix with God, Who was born from thee, the human race, O Mother of God, placeth its joy, and is ever dependent upon thy patronage, and in thee alone hath refuge and defense, who hast full confidence in Him. * * * After the Trinity thou art mistress of all; after the Paraclete, another paraclete; after the Mediator, mediatrix of the whole world."

"How little," writes St. Bonaventura, "can we do in

honor of Mary, since if all our members could become tongues, we should be unable to praise her as she deserves."

As the sorrows of the Mother are reflections of the sufferings of the Son, so the glories of the Lily of Israel are the advance shadows of the divinity of Jesus of Nazareth. We need not fear that our veneration of Mary deprives God the Father of the honor which is properly His, or that our devotion to her as Mediatrix of intercession interferes with our devotion to God the Son as Mediator of redemption. The following beautiful hymn to our Lady by Father Faber well brings out the idea:

"Mother of mercy, day by day
  My love of thee grows more and more.
Thy gifts are strewn upon my way
  Like sands upon the great seashore.
        *   *   *   *   *   *
"But scornful men have coldly said
  Thy love was leading me from God;
And yet in this I did but tread
  The very path my Saviour trod.

"They knew but little of thy worth
  Who spoke these heartless words to me,
For what did Jesus love on earth
  One half so tenderly as thee?

"Jesus, when His three hours were run,
  Bequeathed thee from the Cross to me;
And oh! how can I love thy Son,
  Sweet Mother! if I love not thee?"

Many Protestant writers have drawn inspiration from contemplating the beauties of the Virgin. Edgar Allen Poe invokes her continuous protection in the words:

> "At morn—at noon—at twilight dim—
> Maria! thou hast heard my hymn!
> In joy and woe—in good and ill—
> Mother of God, be with me still!"

The sweet name of Mary has brought forth from Keble, of the *Christian Year*, the following beautiful tribute:

> "Ave Maria! thou whose name
> All but adoring love can claim,
> Yet may we reach thy shrine;
> For He, thy Son and Saviour, vows
> To crown all lowly, lofty brows
> With love and joy like thine."

Even Byron, the greatest of our descriptive poets, though much wrapped up in the contemplation of his own ugly self, yet found time to say of the Immaculate Queen of Heaven:

> "Ave Maria! 'tis the hour of prayer!
> Ave Maria! 'tis the hour of love!
> Ave Maria! my own spirits dare
> Look up to thine and to thy Son above!"

Here is how Mrs. Hemans writes of the Handmaid of the Lord:

> "For such high tidings as to thee were brought,
> Chosen of Heaven! that hour, but thou, O thou!
> E'en as a flower with gracious rains o'er fraught,
> Thy virgin head beneath its crown didst bow
> And take to thy meek breast th' all holy Word,
> And own thyself the Handmaid of the Lord!"

Longfellow, the sweet singer of domestic affection, had too much soul in him not to be enthused by the lowly greatness of the Virgin Mother. He writes:

"This is indeed the Blessed Virgin's land,
  Virgin and mother of our dear Redeemer!
All hearts are touched and softened at her name,
  Alike the bandit with the bloody hand,
The priest, the prince, the scholar and the peasant.
  The man of deeds, the visionary dreamer
Pay homage to her as one ever present!"

Poetry and art, history and literature, pay their tributes to the Virgin; let us give her that religious veneration which so justly belongs to her.

CHAPTER XIII.

THE IMMACULATE CONCEPTION.

THE Canticle of Canticles, one of the most beautiful and poetic compositions in the whole inspired book, represents the love of Christ for His Church—for that Church whose brow time can not wrinkle—and the Liturgy applies this song of Solomon to Mary as the most perfect member of that Church; to her whose love for God is the most ardent, and who is the object of God's own tenderest affection. The words of the Canticle, "Who is she that cometh forth as the morning rising, fair as the moon, bright as the sun?" (Canticle of Canticles vi. 9), convey the highest idea of brilliancy; for they represent her as coming into being fair as the fairest thing that the human mind can conjure up,—as the morning rising, fair as the moon, bright as the sun. It is with her brilliant entry into life, not with her virginity, not with her *privileged* avoidance of sin, not with her long life of merit, not even with her motherhood of God, that we are here concerned. It matters not, says a certain noted preacher, whence we come, but it matters a great deal whither we are going. It matters to us a great deal whence and how Mary came; it matters to us a great deal to get a firm grasp of the doctrine of the Immaculate Conception.

And first of all, what is of faith concerning the Immaculate Conception of the Virgin Mary? "It is a dogma of faith," says the Bull, defining this doctrine, "that the Most Blessed Virgin Mary, in the first instant of her conception, by a singular privilege and grace of God, in virtue of the merits of Jesus Christ, the Saviour of the human race, was preserved from original sin." This proposition in itself and in all its parts is an article of Catholic faith. As day excludes night, as light excludes darkness, so in order to understand immaculateness we must recall to mind something of the nature and the effects of original sin. Our first parent, the gardener Adam, as Tennyson calls him, though constituted in original justice and endowed with many other gifts, such as infused knowledge, immortality, felicity, and freedom from certain temptations, yet gravely violated the one and only commandment imposed upon him by Almighty God. He sinned as representative of the human family, and as such transmitted his sin, with all its ghastly train of evil consequences, including the loss of those benefits with which God had favored him, to all posterity. Hence we are children of a fallen race, stamped with the brand of Satan in our very conception, bearing the sad heritage of original sin and its baneful evils, instead of original justice and its accompanying beauties. For the nature of original sin is the privation from the gaining of that sanctifying grace and justice which ought to be ours according to the order appointed by God. And its effects are concupiscence, disease, a clouded intellect, a will shorn of its strength, and a tendency to the vast and varied kinds of evil. But there is one honorable exception, one lily among the thorns, as some writers love to express it, not because she was freed from original sin by Baptism, as we ordinary mortals are; not because she was sanctified whilst yet unborn, as was St. John the Baptist; but because she was preserved earlier still, namely, from the very moment of her conception; or in other words, when the human soul was united to the body. She was the daughter of a fallen race, and as such was liable to have contracted original sin, and it was by a singular privilege and grace of God that she was exempted from the common doom. For the sake of Him that was to be born of her, and for "His merits foreseen," grace was poured into her soul at the first moment of its being. He who redeemed us redeemed her. Yet her sinlessness differed vastly from the sinlessness of the human soul of Jesus. Bossuet points out the difference. Addressing Christ he says: "Thou are innocent by nature, Mary by grace; thou by excellence, she only by privilege; thou as Redeemer, she as the first of those whom thy precious blood has purified."

This is the doctrine of the Immaculate Conception. There is nothing in it to shock the sensibilities of anybody. There is everything in it to recommend it to the minds and hearts of the faithful. There is nothing in it to justify or even to give a shadow of excuse for those sayings of men in high places, that the latter-day extravagant assumptions of the Catholic Church are intolerable, or, as Frederic Harrison, the arch-apostle of materialism, declares, that her doctrines are outside the pale of legitimate discussion. There is nothing in it to show cause for that mighty clamor raised, as though the social fabric were shaken to its very center, when Pius the Ninth, on the morning of the 8th of December, 1854, defined the doctrine of the Immaculate Conception—a furor kept up until it was diverted by a more important definition, the dogma of Papal Infallibility.

It is well to be able to give a reason for the faith that is in us. The Scripture oracles tell us, at least impliedly, of Mary's immaculateness even to her conception. "I will put enmities," says God, addressing the serpent," between thee and the woman, and thy seed and her seed; she shall crush thy head, and thou shalt lie in wait for her heel" (Gen. iii. 15). The woman spoken of in this passage is Mary, the seed of the woman is Jesus, the serpent is Satan, and the seed of the serpent is sin. The enmity spoken of is not a mere passing one. There was no cessation or shadow of cessation of hostilities between the parties engaged in the conflict. The war is still being waged, and will and must go on to the very end. And as it goes on to the end, so, on the other hand, does it extend back to the beginning. But if there ever was a time when Mary was stained even with original sin, then these hostilities would have ceased, Mary would have been found in the camp of the enemy, and the Scripture would have been falsified. "I will put enmities between thy seed and her seed," continues the voice of God. No one will deny that the enmity between Mary's offspring, that is, Jesus Christ, and Satan's offspring, that is, sin, was perpetual and absolute; yet the very same hostility existed between Mary and Satan, which could not have been the case if she were soiled by sin even for a moment.

This glorious and complete triumph of the Virgin over Satan by the merits of her Son, was promised by God shortly after the fall of our first parents, and was proclaimed and typified in many ways. A type of her immaculateness is seen in the Ark of Noah that escaped the common shipwreck, in the garden fenced round about that can suffer no injury, in that bright city of

God whose foundations are in the Holy Mountains. "Blessed art thou amongst women," are words addressed to her long ago on a very memorable occasion. Such words would have been misused if she were so far inferior to Eve as original sin is to original justice.

The name, "Full of Grace," is her distinguishing and peculiar title, such as our Saviour is called the Just One, or Solomon the Wise One. It is true that the phrase, "Full of Grace," is applied to our Lord by St. John, and to St. Stephen by St. Paul, but this plenitude of grace must be understood, having due regard to persons. The plenitude of grace in Christ is the fullness of an inexhaustible fountain; in Mary, it is the fullness of a great river near the source; in St. Stephen, it is the fullness required for him as a minister and witness of God; in all others, it is the fullness of sufficiency, the rivulets sharing it in a limited degree, yet enough to procure the salvation of all. As applied to Mary, it is the fullness of grace proportionate to her dignity of being the Mother of God. There is no limit to the period past, and hence in her it implies that she was full of grace from the very first moment of her conception.

One may dispute the meaning or question the application of a text, or the authenticity of a word, but there is no room for dispute and no opportunity for cavil in the unanimity with which the Fathers of the Church have held and taught the Immaculate Conception, and that at a time when all admitted that she was the One Holy Catholic and Apostolic Church. So that, if we find the early Fathers of the Church teaching the Immaculate Conception, and in a way which furnishes us with grounds for believing that the doctrine is coëval with the foundation of the Apostolic Church, it is hardly fair to say that it was heard of for the first time in the middle ages. One class of Fathers expounds the words of Genesis, " I will put enmities between thee and the woman," etc., as clearly pointing out immunity from original sin on the part of the Virgin Mary.

Another class is composed of those who, from explaining the Angelic Salutation, " Hail, full of Grace ! " show that what is healed in us by Baptism is stopped in Mary by privilege. To this class belongs St. John Damascene, who writes : " Hail, truly full of grace, hail, since thou art holier than the angels, and more illustrious than the archangels. Hail, full of grace, who art superior to the principalities, sublimer than the powers, more beautiful than the seraphim, higher than the heavens, purer than the sun which we look upon."

A third class teaches it not in express terms but in equivalents, which go to show the independence and truthfulness of their teaching.

Yet another class of the Fathers shows this doctrine by instituting a comparison between our first parents and Mary. The comparisons between immaculate earth and the Immaculate Virgin, between Eve whilst yet immaculate or unstained by original sin and the Blessed Virgin Mary, between Eve before her fall and Mary in her office of the Incarnation, are almost commonplaces of patristic literature and theology. That she is the second Eve, that she untied the knot of Eve's disobedience, the builders of the primitive Church tell us again and again, so that we may reasonably ask the question, Was she not as favored as Eve ? And she would not be, had she been stained with original sin.

St. Augustine and St. Jerome may be looked upon as the two great exponents in their time of the doctrine of the Eastern and Western Church respectively. The former writes: "By a woman, life, by a woman, death;" whilst the latter expresses it, "Death by Eve, life by Mary." Perhaps the clearest of all patristic evidence is given by St. Ephraim: "Two were made, simple, innocent, perfectly like each other, Mary and Eve, but afterwards one became the cause of our death, the other of our life." The whole tone and trend of their writings go to show that Mary came to undo the mischief which Eve had done, and for this it would never do if she had been inferior to Eve in her conception, so that although Eve afterwards fell and though Mary was the child of a fallen race, liable to contract orginal sin, yet, as St. Sedulius puts it, "She came all sinless from the sinful stem of Eve, * * * as the rose springs from the rugged thorn."

There is scarcely any doctrine which the faithful embraced and adhered to with such loving reverence as that of the Immaculate Conception. Although it was taught by the early Fathers of the Church, yet there existed no controversy about it until the days of St. Bernard, the last of the Fathers. And as discussion quickened investigation, men began to learn that from time immemorial the Church had been celebrating a festival of the Immaculate Conception; that the liturgies of the Eastern and Western Church point to an Immaculate Mary; that hymns had been sung in honor of the Immaculate Conception; and that panegyrics had been preached from the earliest times, which supposed and declared this privilege in Mary. When we consider that a Church, which we hold and can prove to be infallible, permitted and approved of all this, what more was to be desired than that the Church should propose formally and solemnly to the faithful a doctrine which for centuries had entered into her every-day life?

And it is fitting, from whatever aspect we view the question, that Mary's conception should have been immaculate. It is fitting, as the great Mediatrix between sinners and God, that she had never been displeasing to Him. It is fitting, as crusher of the serpant's head, that she had never been under the control of Satan. It is fitting, as the cherished child of God the Father, that He should have possessed her "from the beginning of her way." It is fitting, as Spouse of the Holy Ghost, that she should have been as sinless as God could create her. It is eminently fitting, as Mother of Jesus Christ, that she had always been without spot or stain. For were it otherwise, then Lucifer would have had the laugh against Jesus, and could point out that things had taken a strange turn, that a time was when the Virgin was nothing to be proud of, a time was when she was fit company for the demon himself, so that, in order to save the Son from humiliation, it was necessary that the mother should have been immaculate.

Suppose we were not aware of this Scriptural testimony, and all this overwhelming evidence of the Fathers, and all the ancient documents, and monuments, and liturgies, and practices, which point unmistakably to the belief of the early Church, and all this fitness arising from Mary's grand destiny as mother of Christ, as favorite child of God the Father, and as mystic spouse of God the Holy Ghost: yet the word of the infallible Church declaring Mary to be Queen conceived without original sin, is sufficient for us.

Devotion to our Blessed Lady has a special claim on us here in America, for it goes hand in hand with the spread of the Church. And this is true in a marked manner of the propagation of Catholicity in this country. A chapter of the history of our first missionaries is a chaplet of devotion to Mary Immaculate. When our own Marquette first conceived the idea of coming here, he prayed long and fervently to Mary Immaculate that permission might be given him to come to "that populous pagan land through which that mighty river rolled on to the far southern seas."

* * * * * * *

It is consoling amidst the troubled waters of this life, whether annoyed by things social, or things domestic, or things political, that we can always claim the assistance of her who is the comforter of the afflicted. We should not forget her, whether we live in the sunshine of this world's prosperity, or in the winter of its adversity. We honor her because an angel has declared her to be full of grace, and preëminently blessed among women; we honor her because she is the cherished child of God the Father, the much-loved mother of God the Son, made man; we honor her because she is a

> "Woman
> Above all other women glorified,
> Our tainted nature's solitary boast;
> Purer than foam on central ocean tost,
> Fairer than eastern skies at sunset strewn
> With fancied roses."

CHAPTER XIV.

MIXED MARRIAGES.

GOD addressed words of solemn warning to his chosen people in reference to marriage. The words are: "Neither shalt thou make marriages with them. Thou shalt not give thy daughter to his son, nor take his daughter for thy son, for she shall turn thy son from following Me, that he may serve strange gods, and the wrath of the Lord shall be kindled, and will quickly destroy thee" (Deut. vii, 3, 4). The Jews were blessed with the true religion in their day, and lest that religion should be lost or even dulled in their hearts, marriage with unbelievers was forbidden. In other words, mixed marriages were not allowed. Any one who believes that life is a serious business, and not a time to be frittered away on useless things, will easily realize the all-consuming importance of this subject. He will easily see that on well-assorted marriages depends the spiritual and temporal prosperity of the parties concerned; that on them depend the right training, physical and mental, of the children; the teaching of those children to be dutiful sons and daughters, good men and good women, good citizens in this life, and, eventually, citizens of Heaven. He will see that the future of the world, the well-being of society, the progress of mankind, depend largely upon the sanctity of the marriage tie. He will understand, on the other hand, how ill-assorted marriages bring naught save desolation to the household; blight to life's early promise; death to the pleasures of life; all manner of woes to the offspring of such a union; and, perhaps, perpetual ruin in the next life. He will see that though marriages are popularly said to be made in Heaven, some of them bear the impress of Satan upon them. I say these things, not for the purpose of discouraging marriage, for that might be contrary to individual interests, contrary to the interests of the State, contrary to the interests of the Church, contrary to the interests of souls; but I say it in order that people may be induced to use their judgment and to exercise a caution in the selection of a partner, in some way proportionate to the gravity of the question.

We Catholics look upon marriage as a civil contract, that is, a contract to be entered into according to the just laws of the country, having due regard for the temporal concerns of the contracting parties. We look upon marriage as a contract arising from the law of nature, binding the contracting parties to certain duties and obligations, and binding them for life. We also look upon it as a Sacrament of the New Law, and, as such, it requires a careful preparation, such as people make for the reception of any other Sacrament. We look upon marriage as binding the parties for life, not as a thing wherein one may set the other aside, and that, as sometimes happens, for a most trivial reason, such as what is euphemistically called incompatibility of temper; not as something wherein one may repudiate the other, as you throw away a worn-out hat or a threadbare coat; we believe when a Catholic man and a Catholic woman promise in the marriage ceremony to accept each other till death parts them, they mean it; we hold the teaching of Christ on the indissolubility of the bond of Christian marriage, as laid down in His Sermon on the Mount; we accept His conclusion contained in the words: "What God hath joined together let no man put asunder" (Math. xiv, 6). We look upon marriage as a Sacrament, for so the Church considered it even at a time when all admitted her to be the one true Church; so the Scriptures insinuate and the Fathers teach; and the Council of Trent declares it is "truly and properly one of the seven Sacraments of the evangelical law instituted by Christ." We look upon it as a holy Sacrament—holy in its founder, who is Jesus Christ; holy in its signification, for it is a figure of the union of the Divine Word with human nature, a hallowed copy of the union of Christ with His Church, and of the Holy Ghost with the souls of the just; holy in its effects, which are sanctifying and actual graces; holy in the object of its institution, which is to multiply the children of God, and bring them to eternal salvation. These things being so, it is all the more incumbent on people to follow the wisest counsels in selecting partners for life.

It is a well-known fact, and admitted by all jurists, that the Canon Law—the law of the Church—is most wise and just; and the chief excellencies of other codes are to be found when the principles laid down in our Canon Law have been adopted. To the laws of our Church, then, we have to look for the best course to be followed in reference to marriages. She has power to make laws for the good government of her subjects because she is a society; and, as such has power to govern her own members ; and because Christ gave her all powers necessary, or even useful, for the right government of a Christian commonwealth. In the exercise of that power, in order to promote the spiritual, and, indeed, the temporal welfare of the children, she has decreed that there shall be certain impediments to matrimony. The law of nature itself, that is, the law imprinted as it were on our hearts, telling us that certain things are of their own nature good, and therefore ought to be done; and certain things are inherently bad, and therefore to be avoided,—this grand law, coming directly from the Creator's hand, puts certain impediments to marriage. Some impediments make marriage null and void; others render it unlawful, but not invalid. We are dealing with one obstacle only, and that is the difference of religion in the contracting parties.

For all practical purposes, we may describe a mixed marriage to be a marriage between a Catholic and a non-Catholic, whether the latter be baptized or unbaptized. If there be question of an unbaptized person marrying a Catholic without a dispensation, the marriage, according to the discipline of our Church, is null and void. If we mean a marriage between a Catholic and a non-Catholic who is baptized, the marriage is valid, but not lawful, unless a dispensation be obtained from the prohibitory law.

A great deal of misapprehension obtains in reference to mixed marriages. Some seem to think that the opposition of the Church in this matter is a new-fangled idea, whereas, if there be anything clear from ecclesiastical history, it is the stern opposition of the Church in every age against these unhallowed unions. Others imagine, because they have known some cases of mixed marriages to have taken place with ecclesiastical permission, that therefore they are unforbidden. The Church allows mixed marriages in some cases where dispensations from the law have been granted for sufficient reason, but in such cases, and in such only, does she permit them. Some have an idea that it is altogether a matter of discretion for the pastor whether he will marry persons of different religions or not. The truth is this : The pastor has not discretionary powers. The people are bound to observe the laws of the Church ; the pastor is bound to see that they do observe them. We must not be understood as finding fault with our Protestant brethren, when we set our faces against mixed marriages. Why should we find fault with those who follow the dictates of conscience? We believe with the late Dr. Murray, of Maynooth College, who spoke for the Protestants of Ireland, and with Cardinal Newman, who gave his opinion in reference to the sincerity of his Protestant fellow countrymen, and with Dr. Libermann, who might be looked upon as an authority on German Protestantism, that the vast majority of Protestants are in good faith, and they honestly think they are journeying by a safe way to Heaven. But we do find fault with the Catholic who deliberately sets the laws of his Church at defiance, who brings disgrace upon himself and upon his religion, and far-reaching misery upon his offspring. We say, as the marriage of a Catholic with a Protestant is not good for the former, so the marriage of a Catholic with a Protestant is not good for the latter.

Mixed marriages are forbidden by the Sacred Scriptures. The whole drift of God's law in the Old Testament on this subject, from the sixth chapter of Genesis, where we are told the sons of Seth married the daughters of Cain, who were unbelievers, on to the direct prohibition in Deuteronomy, " Neither shalt thou make marriages with them," is one uncompromising protest against these unions. These are forbidden by an ecclesiastical law which is absolute and universal. It is universal, for it extends to all lands and Christian peoples; it is absolute, for it is enacted on the presumption that the danger exists, and therefore, according to the general principle of such laws, it binds even when one may prudently judge that there is no spiritual danger in a particular case; so that even in the absence of all danger, a Catholic contracting such a marriage without a dispensation from the prohibitory law, would be guilty of a grievous sin.

Mixed marriages are forbidden by the law of nature, because of the many and dangerous evils which spring from them. There is, first of all, the danger of perversion or loss of faith. This danger arises from such familiar association as must necessarily exist between man and wife, from non-Catholic books, from the various threats, snares, entreaties, flatteries, that are made use of to effect such a purpose. And if the faith of the Catholic be not always destroyed, it is sometimes made cold and practically dead.

The second danger is, that the children of such a marriage may not be brought up in the Catholic Church. This is no imaginary danger, and everyone knows some sad example of it. All the circumstances of such marriages tend to this result. The difficulty of common prayer, the difficulty of preserving Catholic surroundings in the home, the difficulty as to the fulfillment of religious duties, the evil example of seeing one parent going to one church, the other to another, all show how serious is the danger which threatens the faith of the children of a mixed marriage

The third great danger is that of indifference to all religion. Mixed marriages foster indifferentism—the great bane of the age. They tend to make people forget the Divine Commission, "preach the Gospel to every creature." Christ did not mean that the Apostles should preach any Gospel which their fancy might suggest, but He meant "whatsoever I have commanded you." They incline people to the belief that one religion is as good as another—a belief which is in direct opposition to the old creed drawn up by the Apostles, in which we say, "I believe in the Holy Ghost, the Holy Catholic Church."

The fourth danger is that of dissensions in the family circle. For a true Christian marriage, grace should meet grace, and Faith should be united with Faith. Even the very minds should be married, and to the union of true minds there should be no obstacle. A harmony of souls is necessary for happiness. There are causes enough for disagreement between husband and wife without adding a needless one—that of difference of religion. The man who, as a wooer, or a lover, is all sweetness, may as a husband have very little respect or even toleration for his wife's religious opinions.

The next great danger arises from this, lest the Catholic should die and thus leave the children exposed to the almost moral certainty of being brought up in another faith, or worse still, without any belief whatever. Catholics who incur this risk, run counter to the teachings of St. Paul in the words: "If any have not care of his own, and especially of those of his house, he hath denied the Faith and is worse than an infidel" (I. Tim. v. 8). Non-Catholics who believe they can be saved as easily in one church as in another, may not see the point of this. But Catholics who believe in the one true Church, who have no reason and no room for doubt, who know the truth and can give a reason for their faith, are the ones who are reprehensible if they willingly expose themselves to these dangers.

There is yet another danger. It is that of divorce. We believe that the marriage tie cannot be broken; we hold that no court of justice can separate those whom God has joined. Not so, however, with our separated brethren. In not a few of our States and Territories divorce is granted for many and trivial causes, causes so trifling as to promote merriment if the subject were not so serious. With divorce comes blighted hopes, withered prospects, disappointed affections, and all the ills that follow in the train of a ruined home.

And even though all these dangers be absent, yet a dispensation from the law of the Church is necessary—a dispensation never given without a grave cause, and generally in order to prevent greater evils. Whatever reasons may have existed in the past, it is seldom, in the present circumstances of this country, and with the necessary number of Catholics, that we find solid reasons to justify such marriages. Before a dispensation from the prohibitory law can be obtained, the non-Catholic party must make certain promises in writing and in presence of witnesses. The non-Catholic must promise:

First, to allow the Catholic full liberty of conscience in the exercise of Catholicity.

Second, that all the children shall be baptized, and

brought up in the Catholic Church. Even though all this were done, though a sufficient cause existed for a dispensation, though the required promises were made, though the parties were married before the priest, how many are there who keep their word thus solemnly pledged? Those who are in a position to know, those whose daily life brings them in contact with mixed marriages and their results, tell us that the number who break their promises in this matter is simply astonishing. Nor can they be compelled by law to keep them, for it would appear that ante-nuptial promises are, in point of law, entirely void. Bishop Ullathorne presents this aspect of the question with great clearness and force. "It would be unjust," he writes, " as well as ungenerous, not to admit that there are Protestants who loyally keep the promises they have made in marriage with Catholics, and who truly respect the faith and religious exercises of their Catholic spouse, and fulfill their pledges respecting the education of the children. But prudence looks to what generally happens, and not to the exceptional cases, and wisdom never runs any serious risks in matters of the soul. The individuals, and even the families, that have fallen from the Church through mixed marriages, amount to numbers incredible to those who have not examined the question thoroughly; and the number of Catholics bound at this moment in mixed marriages, who live in a hard and bitter conflict for the exercise of their religion, for that of their children, and, in certain cases, for the soundness of their moral life, could they, with all the facts, be known, would deter any thoughtful Catholic from contracting a mixed marriage."

These are the chief reasons why the Church is

opposed to mixed marriages. Her very ceremonial and ritual for mixed marriages bring out this opposition in stronger relief. A mixed marriage can not take place in the Church. There can be no nuptial Mass and no marriage blessing. The priest is present, but only as an official witness. He is not there to impart a blessing, and he does not pray for them in the name of God's Church. The ceremonial is deprived of the beautiful liturgy, and everything about it is more suggestive of a funeral than a marriage.

But in order to prevent the effects we must remove the causes. Foremost amongst the causes of mixed marriages is a lack of serious reflection. People entail upon themselves and upon others untold misery because they will not think. Their thoughtlessness reminds us of the words of Jeremiah: "With desolation is the land made desolate, because there is no one that considereth in his heart." If a man build a house or buy a horse, he will consult with those who are better informed than himself; but if he be about to contract a mixed marriage he will not stop to consider its consequences, nor pause to find out its dangers from those whose duty it is to know. A second cause of mixed marriage is lack of strong faith. The Church is the exponent of revealed truth, and the director of our actions. Now, if people had a lively faith in the Church of God, and would only realize the antagonism of the Church to such marriages, they would never think of contracting them.

Other causes of mixed marriages are the absence of religious education; the neglect of the Sacraments in early manhood and womanhood; the bad example of others; the absurd idea that Catholics, because of their religious principles, are socially inferior to non-Catholics;

and the silly literature of the time. We refer in particular to the modern novel, for whilst novel-writing has very much degenerated of late, there are other departments of literature in which there are writers equal to those of any period, and more numerous than they have ever been since the dawn of English literature. There is yet another cause, and it is this: Young people sometimes put themselves in such social intercourse that passionate fancy and youthful thoughtlessness are likely to bring about these mischievous unions. There is no effect without a cause. Take away the causes and the effects will stop.

People should take heed lest they be led into a labyrinth of misery by mixed marriages. There is no need to marry a Philistine. There is no need of running the risk of being treated as poor old Samson, the giant, was; or as Socrates, the philosopher, was; or as Job, that time-honored example of patience, was; or as John Ruskin, the great art-critic, was treated. If people marry for money, the partner is usually an incumbrance; if they marry for convenience, it usually turns out to be an inconvenience; if they marry for position they seldom attain it, for that is acquired by merit, not by matrimony.

CHAPTER XV.

DIVORCE.

SOME social reformers, and some journalists, seem to think that the question of divorce is not of much practical moment for Catholics. With this opinion we beg respectfully to differ. An idea has its history, its rise, growth, and development, as well as an individual. Catholics are interested in the social and religious wellbeing of their non-Catholic brethren. As long as Catholics form part of the body politic, as long as they are interested in the welfare of the community, thus long will the subject of divorce have a practical utility for them.

The words of the ritual used by the bride and bridegroom on their wedding day point out the nature of the marriage tie. They make a promise not restricted by any definite period; for it is to last till death. The bridegroom says: "I take thee to be my wedded wife, to have and to hold from this day forward, for better, for worse, for richer, for poorer, in sickness and in health, till death do us part, if holy Church will it permit; and thereto I plight thee my troth." The bride uses a like form. These words are full of meaning. They take each other for better, for worse. No matter what ills may come, the undertaking is irrevocable. They take each other for richer, for poorer.

Even though the winter of adversity should come upon them, that solemn undertaking is still unbroken. They take each other in sickness and in health. Though disease may leave its rough hand on the once fair face and faultless form, still the words of the wedding day must be kept inviolable. Death, and death only, can sever the tie. Other contracts may be broken, but once a Christian marriage is completed it lasts till death. Friends may tread different paths of life; brothers may leave the old roof-tree; merchants may dissolve partnership; nations may set aside treaties; but once married, married till death. Other contracts derive their binding force from the will of the contracting parties, or from the human laws which sanction them. The contracting parties may set aside their own conditions by mutual consent, but not so with the matrimonial contract; for it is of Divine authorship and God has determined its conditions.

The first essential condition of the matrimonial contract is unity. It has been so from the beginning. God Himself, by creating one wife for Adam, sanctioned the unity of marriage and condemned polygamy. But He did more. He confirmed His act by His words when He said: "Wherefore a man shall leave father and mother and shall cleave to his wife, and they shall be two in one flesh" (Gen. ii. 24). He does not say they shall be three, or four, or five, or six in one, such as those at Salt Lake City attempt. Mormonism is a great blotch on the fair face of this Republic. More dangerous, because more respectable, is the subject we are considering—divorce.

Public opinion in this country is strongly opposed to Mormonism, and yet with a strange inconsistency, there is no such Christian sentiment against divorce. The latter is just as much at variance with the proper ends of marriage as the former. Divorce differs not substantially from Mormonism. The difference is, that whilst Mormonism permits a man to have several wives at once, divorce practically allows him to have as many as he pleases, but one after another, and whilst the previous wives still live. The annals of the divorce court are a sad commentary on the morals of the nation. Mathew Arnold, writing of the English divorce court, says it is an institution which neither makes divorce impossible nor makes it decent; which allows a man to get rid of his wife, or a wife of her husband, but first makes them drag one another through a mire of unutterable infamy. "When," he continues, "one looks on this charming institution, with its crowded benches, its newspaper reports, and its money compensations—this institution in which the gross British Philistine has stamped an image of himself—one may be permitted to find the marriage theory of Catholicism refreshing and invigorating." If he were to write of the American divorce court his language would be much stronger. To make confusion more confounded, the laws of the States differ enormously as to the legal causes of divorce. Some one has pointed out that a man traveling from Maine to Louisiana may come under the operations of fourteen different laws upon the subject of divorce. In one State he may be free to wed, in another a married man, whilst in a third he may be prosecuted for bigamy. The laws of the United States on the subject of divorce are a monument of stupidity, and yet there is little or no effort made by any religious denomination to improve this miserable state of affairs, except what is being done by the Catholic Church.

Those who claim to be Christians, no matter to what religious denomination they belong, should follow the law of Christ on the subject of divorce. The three Evangelists, Matthew, Mark, Luke, and a still greater teacher than any of these, Paul of the Gentiles, tell us of that law. We shall first take the account given in the nineteenth chapter of St. Matthew. For a proper understanding of it, we must remember the circumstances that called forth from Christ this defense of the marriage tie. Amongst the Jews there were two great parties, half political, half religious. One of their subjects of controversy was the cause of divorce. Some of the Pharisees, or representatives of one of the great parties above mentioned, came to Jesus and asked Him: "Is it lawful for a man to put away his wife for any cause whatever?" Christ treats the question with a gentle, wholesome irony. "Have ye not read," He answers, "that He who made man from the beginning, made them male and female?" His words to them are a rebuke, because they, men versed in the law, men supposed to be conversant with the sacred Scriptures, should have known the original idea of marriage. Christ continues: "For this cause shall a man leave father and mother and cleave to his wife, and they shall be two in one flesh. Therefore now they are not two but one flesh. What therefore God hath joined together let no man put asunder" (3–5). The words of Christ are clear. They are a solemn prohibition making the marriage of Christians indissoluble after its consummation. This is the law laid down by Christ, not in a discourse on ideals, but in reply to a question relative to divorce. And yet the acts of our law-makers are such that we can not help recalling the words of England's greatest poet :

> " Man, proud man
> Dressed in a little brief authority:
> Most ignorant of what he's most assured,
> His glassy essence—like an angry ape,
> Plays such fantastic tricks before high heaven
> As make the angels weep."

Not content with this explanation, His querists raise an objection and ask : "Why then did Moses command to give a bill of divorce, and to put away ?" (7). Moses was a great and God-fearing man, a leader of the chosen people, and he would not willingly command a wrong. Christ's answer puts the matter in the clearest light. Moses as a law-giver did not introduce divorce amongst his people. He did not order a bill of divorce. His action is somewhat illustrated by the case of a man who suffers from a perplexed conscience. The perplexed soul imagines a sin is committed, whether an action is performed or is not; that there is no way of avoiding sin in a particular case. If the perplexity can not be removed by prayer, by consultation, or such like means, there is no sin committed in selecting that which seems to be the less of two evils. Christ denies that Moses ordered a divorce. He permitted or tolerated it because of the hardness of their hearts ; he permitted it because otherwise that stiff-necked people would have fallen into greater crimes ; he permitted it because there was great danger that, had he not done so, these men would rid themselves by murder of their hated wives. Christ takes this opportunity of reminding them that it was not always so ;

that under the gospel of peace and love which He came to preach, the original state of matrimony should be restored. "He saith to them: Because Moses by reason of the hardness of your hearts permitted you to put away your wives, but from the beginning it was not so. And I say to you, that whosoever shall put away his wife, except it be for fornication, committeth adultery, and he that shall marry her that is put away, committeth adultery" (8, 9). By reason of the exception mentioned in the foregoing text, some Protestants contend that it is lawful for a man to obtain a divorce with permission to re-marry. But it is an acknowledged canon of biblical and indeed historical criticism, that a text must be read in the light thrown upon it by other texts. We turn to the pages of Mark, Luke, and Paul for this light. In the tenth chapter of St. Mark we read: "Whosoever shall put away his wife and marry another, committeth adultery upon her. And if the wife shall put away her husband and be married to another, she committeth adultery" (11, 12). The words of St. Luke are equally clear. "Every one who putteth away his wife and marrieth another, committeth adultery; and he that marrieth her that is put away from her husband, committeth adultry" (xvi. 18). The evidence of St. Paul is: "But to them that are married, not I but the Lord commandeth, that the wife depart not from her husband. And if she depart, that she remain unmarried, or be reconciled to her husband. And let not the husband put away his wife" (I. Cor. vii. 10, 11). St. Jerome is one of the greatest Scriptural scholars of the Christian Church. Therefore we must not overlook his explanation. He writes: "Because it might happen that a woman be accused wrongfully, and that a man would make the charge in order to pass to a second marriage, he is allowed to dismiss his wife on condition that he shall have no other in her lifetime."

The Catholic Church, relying on the words of sacred Scripture and of the Fathers, will give a divorce from bed and board when there is a just cause, but will not and can not give permission to either party to marry another. This is also a partial answer to those who say that the teaching of our Church exacts too much from poor, suffering humanity. What if there be some cases of individual suffering? The answer is complete if we recall the principle, that because a law is inconvenient in some of its special applications it must not therefore be suppressed. The general happiness of the married life is secured by its indissolubility, and when people know they must live together this very necessity makes them try to lighten the burdens of married state.

The union of husband and wife is compared to that of Christ and His Church. Christ must always remain with the Church; marriage is a type of never-ending union. In his Epistle to the Ephesians, St. Paul says: "Husbands, love your wives, as Christ also loved the Church, and delivered Himself up for it, that He might sanctify it, cleansing it by the laver of water in the word of life, that He might present it to Himself a glorious Church, not having spot nor wrinkle, or any such thing, but that it should be holy and without blemish. So also ought men to love their wives as their own bodies. . . . . . For this cause shall a man leave his father and mother, and shall cleave to his wife, and they shall be two in one flesh" (v. 25–31).

Divorce is a fruitful source of endless crimes. The

principle of divorce is a principle of decadence. Its sanction prompts men and women to commit crime; its presence produces an inferior and degraded womanhood; it hinders the education of children; it sets families at variance; it scoffs at all that is purest and truest in humanity; and the lesson of history is that wide-spread divorce is invariably connected with national decay. Every man in the land, for the sake of his family, for the sake of his common humanity, for the sake of his country and of his God, should set his face against this social cancer. Every woman also, should do her share to stamp out the evil. Divorce affects woman more injuriously than man. As long as the vigor of youth and the glow of beauty are hers, she may be safe; but when they have disappeared, when the tempter is nigh, when a man knows he can get a divorce, then is the danger that she will be dethroned from her place as queen of the household where the law of Christianity has placed her.

In the days of Paganism the wife was either the toy or the slave of her husband. One day she was favored, the next she was turned adrift like a hireling. Matters came to such a pass in Pagan Rome that women counted their years by the number of their husbands; family life was practically at an end; propagation of the race was stopped among the old Roman families; and, lest the race should come to an end, the State found it necessary to offer premiums for the birth of children. But Christianity reëstablished the family, enforced the indissoluble union of the marriage bond, and put the wife in the place of honor in the household. It made her be respected in her old age as well as in youth; in faded loveliness as in all the wild freshness of morn.

No one can deny that at the door of Protestantism is to be laid the modern evils of divorce. Mr. T. D. Woolsey, himself a Protestant, in his book on "Divorce and Divorce Legislation," says: "The leaders in the changes of matrimonial law were the Protestant reformers themselves, and that almost from the beginning of the movement. . . . . . The reformers, when they discarded the sacramental view of marriage and the celibacy of the clergy, had to make a new doctrine of marriage and divorce." Luther and Melancthon allowed Philip of Hesse to have two wives at the same time. Cranmer, the first primate of the Protestant Church in England, granted Henry the Eighth a divorce from his lawful wife, the pious Catherine of Arragon. If the Catholic Church had acted similarly, what would have become of the condensed civilization of all the ages to which we are the rightful heirs? We should have sunk to the level of some of the barbarous nations of Asia, and the Mongolian of to-day might be held up to us as a model of culture. To her honor be it said, her Pontiffs have always done battle for civilization and society. Pope Nicholas the First espoused the cause of the queen against her husband, King Lothaire of Lorraine. His successor, Adrian II., defended her just cause with equal vigor. Urban II. excommunicated Philip of France for having put away his wife and living with the wife of the Count of Anjou. Innocent III. compelled Philip Augustus to take back his wife. Gregory the Seventh defied the anger of Henry the Fourth of Germany in defense of a wronged and banished wife. Clement the Seventh refused to abandon the cause of Catherine of Arragon against her husband, Henry the Eighth, even though by his action he lost all England to the Church. The causes, ethical, social, and legal, of divorce are many; the remedy is to be found in impressing upon society the sacramental idea of matrimony, the teaching of the Catholic Church.

Divorce from bed and board is somewhat of a remedy for those who find, alas! too late, that they can not live together. The Catholic Church allows this when there is a justifying cause. The final and decretive remedy must come from that Church which holds the clear and literal meaning of the words: "What therefore God hath joined together let no man put asunder" (Mark x. 9).

CHAPTER XVI.

IS THERE A LIFE BEYOND THE GRAVE?

"THE soul is the principle of life." So said Aristotle, and after him St. Thomas, who purified, christianized, and divested of its oriental coloring, the philosophy of the former. A stone, for example, has no life; it is not capable of motion from within. It has existence, and this we have in common with it. But we have more than mere existence, and in order to understand how much more, we must distinguish between the vegetative soul, the sensitive or perceptive, and the rational soul. A plant is capable of absorption and has a vegetable life or soul; a brute has this also, but has in addition a sensitive or perceptive soul. The soul of man embraces all, for it is vegetative, sensitive, and rational. The vital principle of plants and animals is dependent on matter; not so with the soul. Its spirituality distinguishes it from things below us, its union with the body marks it off from pure spirits, the angels or things above us, for they are bodyless. Man thinks, and wills, and reasons. Every one knows that he can think, will, reason, reflect, etc. These are acts of the soul, for the body can not perform them. They point to a spiritual principle within us, because matter is incapable of such acts. Spiritual things have their phenomena as well as physical things. Thought, wish, action, and such like, are the phenomena of the soul; they point to the substance from which they come, such as inertness, extension, quantity, lead us to the things which support them. We must not, therefore, be surprised to read in Genesis: "God having made man of the slime of the earth, breathed on his face the breath of life and man became a living soul" (ii. 7). Our position thus far then is this: The soul exists. It has an existence apart from matter, and an action in which the body takes no part.

The following words of Professor Tyndall are the expression of a certain school of thought: "Whither go we? The question dies without an answer, without even an echo, upon the infinite shores of the unkown. * * * * Having exhausted physics and reached its very rim, the real mystery still looms up beyond us. We have, in fact, made no step toward its solution. And thus it will ever loom, even beyond the bourne of knowledge, compelling the philosophies of successive ages to confess that

'We are such stuff
As dreams are made of, and our little life
Is rounded with a sleep.'"

Physics can not answer the question, for the reason that it is outside its pale. Philosophy gives a reasonable answer, Christianity puts it beyond all doubt. The advanced materialist says, everything which exists is matter; the more moderate materialist admits the existence of an uncreated spirit, but created spirits are to him creatures of the imagination. He heeds not the workings nor the warnings of the spirit within him. The medical materialist tells us of the number of bodies he has examined and dissected, and that in all his examinations and dissections he could not perceive a soul. Can you see the magnetism in the needle, or the undischarged electricity in the cloud? No; but you can see these phenomena such as you can see the phenomena of soul, and we are as justified in reasoning up to the existence of the one as to that of the other. The materialist does not find the soul because he starts out with the conclusion that it does not exist, and his method of investigation does not lead to it. Whilst he follows this system of search, it is as easy and as likely for the grave-digger to reach the stars as for the materialist to find the soul.

The nature of the human soul opens up to the mind a sphere full of unseen beauty and loveliness. The soul is a spiritual substance, and in this we discern one likeness between it and the Creator. It can form a judgment and can compare ideas; such would be impossible if the soul were not spiritual. Mere matter is incapable of comparing ideas and therefore of forming a judgment. The soul is capable of abstract ideas. It can form its own thoughts and make them the subject of other thoughts. Those statements need no proof, for any one with the use of reason may test them. The attributes of the will point unmistakably to the spirituality of the soul.

The soul is free; experience teaches its freedom. There is no insuperable necessity to do something or to avoid something. We can avoid evil; we may do good. The will is somewhat shackled by reason of man's fall, but it is free and responsible nevertheless. The ideas of justice and injustice, of virtue and vice, establish the liberty of the soul. All distinguish between natural defects and vice; between acts done without deliberation and those that are premeditated. The distinction would be meaningless if the soul were not free. Without liberty there is no merit.

The unanimous consent of all peoples tells us of the freedom of the soul. Such a consent, provided it has the requisite conditions, is a sure motive of judging. That there exists this unanimity of consent is clear from the laws, precepts, councils, exhortations, praise, blame, reward, punishment, which obtain among all nations. These would be absurd if man were not a free agent. The unanimity of consent regarding the freedom of the soul is of the greatest importance, and is opposed to the evil inclinations of man. If the soul were not free God's commandments were ridiculous. The soul then exists, is the principle by which we live, and know, and resolve; is the seat of the acts of sensation, of mind, of will, and of memory; can not be coerced, possesses freedom, and is a spiritual substance.

We claim for it another likeness to its Creator, and it is this which gives us the life beyond the grave, immortality. God says we are created to His own image. He is a pure spirit. Our souls are like unto Him, spiritual beings that can never die. The soul has no parts. It can not be disjointed or disunited, as, for example, a building can. That it has no parts or atoms of any kind we know from many sources, for example, from its power of forming judgment; and that which has no parts can not be destroyed. Being spiritual, it is incorruptible and no created force can destroy it. In its action it is independent of matter; in its being it is equally independent. It is therefore of its own nature incorruptible. The body is constantly changing; the soul, never. Old men remember what they learned in childhood and the friendships of youth are seldom forgotten. It is as easy to corrode electricity as to corrupt the soul in the sense in which we write. Neither from its own nature nor from any created power, then, can destruction come. It is needless to discuss whether God can destroy it or not; for we know that He will not. He tells us again and again that it will live forever. Jesus Christ says: "And there the wicked shall go into everlasting punishment, but the just into life everlasting" (Matt. xxv. 46). Goodness is not always rewarded in this life; nor is wickedness always punished. The noblest deeds of man, patriotism and martyrdom, might pass away unrewarded if there were not a life beyond the grave. God would not be what He is if there were not another life for man. The idea we have of His justice, assuring us that He invariably rewards good and punishes evil, implies another life, because good and evil, virtue and vice, are not always rewarded and punished, respectively, in this life. As the soul is of its own nature indestructible, as it can not be destroyed by any created power, and as God will not destroy it even if He could, the conclusion is that there is a life eternal beyond the tomb.

Let us suppose for a moment that the soul is not immortal and see what absurdities follow. Man, who is looked upon as lord of creation, becomes the veriest puppet and plaything of nature. His innate yearning is never satisfied. Other creatures, supposed to have been created for man's benefit, have their natural tendencies realized in this world; man's aspirations are stunted and his very constitution contains an essential flaw if there be not another life. Such teaching can not stand the test, and man can not be put in a position lower than the brute. Nature can not be false to itself. The impossibility of persuading oneself that he will never again see his departed friends argues a life beyond the grave. "All the subtleties of metaphysics," writes Rousseau, " will not make me doubt the immortality of the soul. I feel it, I wish it, I hope for it, I will defend it with my latest breath."

The history of the human family shows that belief in the immortality of the soul has always obtained among the human race. This belief was frequently disfigured and distorted, yet even in its most hideous form it was capable of being recognized. Modern research has thrown some light on this ancient belief. The graves of Chaldea contain provisions, lamps, etc., which the deceased are supposed to use. That old Egyptian work, "The Book of the Dead," from which the departed are expected to recite in order to get a favorable judgment, points to a belief in the immortality of the soul among that ancient people. The Hebrew race steadfastly, and from the first, adhered to this teaching. Let us look at the Old Testament from a mere historical standpoint, and we find that they held it not as a matter of dispute, but as a firm belief. The belief which runs through all these old books may be expressed in the following words: "It is a holy and a wholesome thought to pray for the dead that they may be released from their sins" (II. Machabees xii. 46). All the old philosophers, such as Plato and Socrates, Cicero and Seneca, Plutarch and Aristotle, proclaimed their belief in another life. Students of Homer and of Virgil know how they expressed the belief of their time by consigning the good after death to the Elysian Fields and the wicked to Hades or Tartarus. The universal belief of the ancient nations is an acknowledged fact of history. All modern peoples, civilized or savage, hold it. Even in the dark continent the Hottentot asks that his bow and arrows be buried with him, so that he may wage war upon his enemies in the next life; and our own Indians have a firm hope of a happy hunting-ground beyond the grave. Belief in the immortality of the soul is now, as it has, ever been, practically the unanimous faith of the human race. The voice of the whole human family is the voice of God. It is a doctrine which is in conformity with man's nature, appeals to his reason, cheats not the mind, and must be true.

There exists in every man a desire, innate and inseparable, of perfect felicity. It is imprinted on his very nature, stamped indelibly on the fleshy tablets of his heart. It is this desire that moves man to action, and by it society is preserved. Coming, as it does, from the great and All-wise Creator of the universe, it can not have been given to us unto mockery and disgrace. But it would be so given if it were never satisfied, and therefore a time must come when this innate and unquenchable desire will be satisfied to its fullest extent. It can not be during this life, because for perfect happiness you require the absence of every evil, the possession of every good, and the certainty of never falling from that state, conditions which it is obvious are unattainable during man's life on earth. Some seek their happiness one way, some another. The gilded youth seeks it in scenes of mirth and sprightliness; the miser seeks it in pressing his money bags close to his heart, in never loosening his purse-strings for any cause, however so

IS THERE A LIFE BEYOND THE GRAVE? 161

good; the epicure seeks it in gratifying his appetite; the ambitious in trying to raise himself to honor, or fortune, or power; the philosopher in solitude and books; but no one finds it. " I have seen and contemplated," writes Cardinal Gibbons, " two of the greatest rulers on the face of the earth,— the civil ruler of sixty-five millions, and the spiritual ruler of two hundred and fifty millions of people. I have conversed with the President and the Pope in their private apartments, and I am convinced that their exalted position, far from satisfying the aspirations of their souls, did but fill them with a profound sense of their grave responsibility."

All have to agree with Solomon, "Vanity of vanities." All are compelled to ask with the distinguished author of Vanity Fair: "Which of us in this life has all that he desires, and having it, is happy?" All have to accept the conclusion of one of the most fascinating philosophers of modern times, "that life for its own sake and without reference to a future state, is not worth the living." Hence we say this desire of perfect felicity, since it has been implanted in our very nature by the hand of God himself; since it can not have been given to us unto mockery and disgrace, and since it can not be satisfied in this life, forces on us the inevitable conclusion that there must be another life in which to satisfy it. In other words, it makes us believe the immortality of the soul. This is the explanation of the "pleasing hope," the "fond desire," the "longing of the immortality." Hence we say, the soul defies the drawn sword. Hence we say, also, the soul will flourish in immortal youth,

> "Unhurt amid the war of elements,
> The wreck of matter and crash of worlds."

"The souls of the just are in the hand of God, and the torment of death shall not touch them. In the sight of the unwise they seemed to die, and their departure was taken for misery. * * * * But they are in peace and their hope is full of immortality" (Wisdom iii. 1-4).

CHAPTER XVII.

READING.

"READING maketh a full man," wrote the philosopher Bacon. On these words we purpose to preach a lay sermon. The body requires drink as well as meat; liquids as well as solids. The soul—the other essential element of human nature—craves for a twofold kind of food ; both kinds spiritual, one of them supernatural, the other may be either natural or supernatural. The supernatural food of the soul is divine grace. Its natural food, since it is that invisible faculty which thinks, is thought. Thought is supplied to us from many sources. We evolve it from our own inner consciousness ; from the world around us ; from the worlds above us ; from God in His creative act ; from God, as seen in things created—trees, flowers, fruits, the whole animal and vegetable worlds—; from God, as seen in the wonderful order of the universe ; from the laws of nature, always unchanged, though occasionally superseded or suspended, as, for instance, in the Gospel miracles ; from the floating knowledge acquired by communication with our fellow-man ; etc., etc. But the great and varied and unfailing supply of food for thought comes from reading. *Read, read, read,* is the advice of St. Augustine of Hippo. The saint meant not omnivorous reading. He knew too well the effects of vicious reading, and its appeal to the passions, sometimes through the intellect, more frequently through the imagination; he knew from sad experience what effects the reading of the lascivious plays of the Roman poet, Publius Terence, had produced in himself before his conversion, to have made his counsel universal.

Under the head of reading we may include newspapers, magazines, periodicals, and books from the slim Seaside Library edition to the ponderous ten-dollar tome.

The power of the press is mighty for good or evil. Like the tongue, it may work a world of iniquity or a world of good. From it may proceed blessing or cursing. Its influence is recognized by all sorts and conditions of men. The clever business-man, be he a banker or a merchant, the shrewd politician, be he a Democrat or a Republican, knowing the power of the newspaper and recognizing its influence, tries to be the proprietor of one, or at least to control it, or to affect it for the advancement of his interest. The apostles of Infidelity and Agnosticism, and the professors of the religion of humanity, have well-regulated and extensively circulating journals at their disposal. "The children of darkness are wiser in their generation than the children of light" (Luke xvi. 8).

The newspaper, be it a daily or a weekly, finds its way into many a home. This is well, provided the paper be good in the ethical sense of the word. But if it be not, how has the parent discharged his duty towards his family? How the obligation of training the young minds of his family? How has he governed his household? Let him think on the words of St.

Paul to Timothy and then supply the answer: "But if any man have not care of his own, and especially those of his own house, he hath denied the faith; he is worse than an infidel" (I. Tim. v. 8).

The literary market is stocked with bad or with worthless newspapers. Take a look at the news-agent's stand and see how it is weighed down with papers that openly attack or sneer at our religion, or what is still more repulsive, patronize it in one paragraph in order to get in a well-directed thrust in the next. The Catholic paper is placed in the background as something seldom asked for. Should the reader desire an illustrated paper, he is supplied with one mainly made up of vile and stupid cartoons of his countrymen, or with one setting forth in its prints deeds of midnight darkness: a robber making his escape on horseback, a female scalding her betrayer with boiling water, a crack shot dealing death around in some gambling den, and such like, that catch hold of the young, and fire their imagination.

And here let us combat one or two objections that we hear in connection with Catholic newspapers. We are told that the paper is no good—not worth buying; that it has too much religion in it and not enough politics; that it advocates the cause of this or that party. It is not worth buying, repeats the fastidious critic. Suppose, for a moment, our Catholic papers be not up to the standard of newspaper excellence, the fault is to be attributed, in great measure, to the apathy of the Catholics themselves. They do not patronize the Catholic press sufficiently well; they do not put the managers of Catholic papers in a position to engage the best talent on our papers. If our papers are not as good as they might be, it is not for lack of talent among Catholic journalists. Many of the leading journalists of this country are Catholics; the leader-writers on most of the London dailies are Catholics; but they are in the hands of non-Catholic employers, and Catholic newspapers have not been able to hold out the pecuniary inducements to enlist this talent on their side. We should say, in the words of the late Archbishop McHale, "If you wish for an honest press you must give in an honest support."

There is too much religion and not enough politics and news in the Catholic papers, is a common plaint against them. Catholic newspapers are not and ought not to be newsy in the sense of chronicling crimes under sensational and fascinating headings, for it is not the part of such journals to cast a halo of romance around the vices of the people, or to screen with a glamour of language the faults and follies of the multitude. And whilst we admit that a Catholic newspaper without politics is like a man without a back-bone—for politics are the public morals of the nation—we do not think that they should take the first place in any Catholic paper. As Catholics, as believers in God, we must hold that everything else must be made subservient to religion, and we believe our Catholics are not so superlatively instructed in their religion but that they might profitably give a few minutes to the reading of an article on a religious subject. We believe a column or two of a newspaper might well be devoted to a short sermon. Then there are the many inexhaustible religio-scientific questions—those questions where science and religion obviously walk hand in hand; those questions where they are apparently, but only apparently, made to clash, for truth can not contradict truth; the various similar questions arising from the innermost recesses of this little planet, onward and upward to the blue arches of heaven. Tell us not that such subjects are unfit for a newspaper and suited only for the pages of a heavy quarterly or a philosophical monthly. Catholics, as a rule, are not so well educated that they can afford to overlook such subjects. Even those who are well informed in their own profession or calling in life, profit not a little by elementary explanations of dogma, of ceremonial, and of questions on science and religion.

Whilst some complain that our Catholic papers have not enough politics in them, others think it a grievance that they should discuss political questions at all. Why Catholic papers should close their columns to politics, it is difficult to understand. The fate and fortunes of Catholicity are not bound to any one party or form of government. A Catholic, as far as Catholicity is concerned, may be a Democrat or a Republican, a Nationalist or a Royalist. Whilst believing in St. Paul's teaching, that there is no power except from God, they do not believe in the divine right of kings. The Catholicity of a country should not be so linked with its form of government that with the latter it must stand or fall. And in those countries where the Church has bound herself thus closely, she has always been the sufferer.

Catholics, as well as other citizens, want to vote, and in some way are bound to do so; and in order to vote intelligently, they must needs have political instruction. There is no reason why they should blindly follow the political teaching of their favorite journal; but in it, and in other papers, they will see the questions at issue discussed, the arguments for and against, and they can draw their own conclusions. Readers of newspapers should learn and practice a little forbearance. A journal advocates the cause of this or that man; at once the reader waxes indignant, stops his subscription, and, in his apparently virtuous indignation, asks how any Catholic can vote for or solicit votes for such a man. A man who votes according to his lights, be they ever so dim, is fully justified in so doing. A journalist is generally a man of eduction, and, as a rule, has more opportunities of being conversant with politics than his readers.

We now come to a more pretentious literature—the magazine. The newspaper and periodical—more particularly the former—are fast pushing books out of the market. It is true John Ruskin reads not newspapers, but in this he has few disciples. Every home wishing to be conversant with the leading questions of the day should have its magazine as well as its newspaper. And here again should be exercised the same watchfulness, so that nothing defiled can enter the sacred precincts of the family circle. Liberty in reading must not degenerate into license. A man having many kinds of food to select from, will not choose that which is poisonous. If the care exercised were proportionate to the excellence of the thing cared for, surely we should be more cautious in providing food for the mind than for the body. The print, paper, style, engravings, may be excellent, but we have to look further. What is the subject-matter? How does it treat religious questions? Does it talk mysteriously about the Unknowable and the religion of Humanity, and dismiss flippantly, if not blasphemously, the most sacred subjects? What is the tone of its historical and scientifico-religious articles? These queries deserve consideration. Select not that magazine which, by its engravings, is suggestive of evil, or by its articles makes moral pitfalls, or raises dogmatic difficulties which your training has not qualified you to solve. Trained theologians are few, and none but these can safely answer the religious difficulties raised in some latter-day magazines. Not that these difficulties are very difficult, for they are generally rehashes of objections, old as the days of the Gnostics; but a man may be well versed in law, or medicine, or business, may know his catechism, may have read religious books not a few, may be a good Christian, and yet be not able to meet such objections. Keep to those magazines that are safe reading. Think not that a man is better informed than you because he happens to have read a magazine article which you may be bound in conscience not to read. We are not advocating the restriction of good reading, but simply the shutting out of that which is bad.

Non-Catholic magazines are gotten up regardless of expense. The highest artistic taste is engaged to render attractive, scenes offensive to pious eyes. The best writers that money can buy are obtained. The workmanship is faultless. There is, or at least there ought to be, as much literary taste and talent among the Catholics of this country as among any of the sects. We believe there is even more artistic taste; and it would indeed be strange and sad were it otherwise, when we consider that our Church has always been the patron of art. Of course, we extend the comparison to the more wealthy only, and proportionate to the numbers of such from the different denominations. The struggle for existence, and even for a competency, is over in many parts, Dame Fortune smiles on not a few, and ease and inclination have given an impetus to literature and art. Hence if our magazines be not equal to those of others, it is because we do not extend that patronage which would enable editors to engage the best talent. For this reason also, non-Catholic magazines are enriched with the fruit of Catholic talent. At the same time we may expect a *quid pro quo*, and not to have to buy the magazine from a sole motive of duty. Give the Catholic periodical a better support, and it will supply better material.

Although papers and periodicals encroach considerably on the domain of books, yet men of higher education and of laudable ambition, people of delicate health, people living in a climate where out-door exercise is somewhat restricted, people wishing to overcome *ennui*, people desirous of being well informed, will read books. Desultory reading is not at all desirable. Give your reading a certain direction; fine out what particular subject you have a taste for; take to it, and you will find pleasure in mastering even its details, and you will know something of kindred subjects; for there is none that stands so severely alone as not to run into other questions. But we are viewing reading from a Catholic standpoint. We are not free to roam at will, regardless of the moral tone of the book. There is hardly anything wherein liberty degenerates so easily into license as in reading. We are apt to lose sight of the ethics of reading, quieting, or smothering, or trying to resist the remonstrances of a good conscience in the light of so-called intellectual culture. Those books that are dangerous to faith or morals are forbidden, as well as those that are positively bad. Some books are prohibited by the natural law, that is, by an ordinance imposed on us by Almighty God and made known to us by the light of reason, telling us that some things are bad in themselves and are to be avoided; commanding other things that are good and necessary for the probity of morals. Of the vices opposed to fraternal charity, scandal is one; and of all kinds of scandal there is none to be more execrated than that begotten of impious and obscene books. Here is what Father Gury, one of the first moral theologians of the nineteenth century, teaches concerning bad books: "This is a diabolical invention, and of all, the most efficacious for hurling whole troops of souls into the pit of hell. It is a plague, the most dreadful and inhuman of all, which affects not only one region or age, but extends to all times and places, and in all makes fearful havoc. Who can tell what dreadful evils to religion and morals have arisen from bad books as from a poisoned fountain, and, indeed will be propagated and multiplied till the end of the world." Obscene books are not permitted to be read by any one. There is not and there can not be any justification for reading them; nor is it lawful to print, or to propagate, or to sell such books. It is sadly amusing to see a group of young men in a railway-car, evidently acquaintances, perhaps friends, reading books so obscene that for very shame one will not allow another to know what he is reading.

Books opposed to faith are also forbidden. Some men, prudent and learned, may be permitted to read them for the purpose of refutation; but then the number is limited, and is generally confined to those who have received a special training in the theological sciences. Our people, as a rule, are not allowed to read such books. A desire to know the other side is not a justifying cause for exposing themselves to the danger of suffering shipwreck of the faith. At the same time we must not be understood as implying that people should not read any book written by a non-Catholic. Perhaps some of the most successful defenses of Christianity have been written in these latter days by non-Catholics. We do not say the most learned or the most logical, but the most successful. In this connection we might mention, "Is Life Worth Living?" by W. H. Mallock, a book in which the author shows that life for its own sake, and without reference to a future state, is not worth living. "Ben-Hur" is another example, good as gold, readable as a romance, sparkling with the purest Christianity.

Education among English-speaking Catholics was for a long time proscribed, and they were insulted because of the faults and follies of their foes. They were deprived of the means of education, and then called ignorant. One may as justly call a man a pauper after having robbed him. Now that those times have passed away, and, in fact, never existed in this country, it is our duty, and it ought to be our pride, to be leaders in intellectual culture, as well as in faith, morality, and social reform. How are we to know whether or not a book is fit to be read? There is little difficulty in answering the question as far as Catholic publications are concerned. Should it treat professedly of some theological subject, it bears the *imprimatur* of the Ordinary who has examined the book, either personally or by deputy. This is a sufficient guarantee of the orthodoxy of the book, though not always of its literary excellence. Young men sometimes desire, and very laudably, too, a more elaborate and lengthened explanation and proof of Catholic doctrine than that contained in our catechisms. There are books not a few, and periodicals many, that contain such admirable explanations of questions and defenses of doctrine, and answers to objections, but since they are for the most part professional, they are known generally only to priests. The pastor, then, or the spiritual director, is the person to be consulted on this point. The main difficulty arises with that class of books known as novels; not those professedly immoral, for they carry with them their own condemnation. Some few prudish people speak as though all novels were bad and should be ostracized. It would be a sad day and lonely to lovers of letters if "Fabiola," "Calista," "Loss and Gain," the charming historical novels of Walter Scott, the delightful pen-pictures of human life by William M. Thackeray, and such similar productions, were set aside by this sweeping denunciation of all books denominated novels. The fact is, outside those books that are intrinsically evil, no very general rule can be given. Some people may read sentimental books as much unmoved as though they were reading the Abbé Darre's treatise on "Trigonometry," or Darwin's work on "Worms." To others of a different temperament and a more vivid imagination, such books may be positively dangerous. Many cases require individual decision, and though universal or even general rules can not be laid down, yet we can find some convenient formulas that will apply to a considerable number of cases. Charles Sante Foi advises people never to read a book descriptive of scenes that they would not look at, or containing words they would not utter. People sometimes read descriptions of scenes and circumstances that they would blush to look at, and peruse without remorse, words that they would resent if orally addressed to them. As it is as sinful to tell a lie on paper as by mouth, so it is as sinful to listen to double-meaning and wickedly-suggestive language through the medium of books as to the spoken word. Some may think the following advice of Charles Sante Foi quite too rigid; however, it is worth noting: " If you would place the moral merit of a book beyond question, ask yourself if you would like to have its author for your spiritual director; do not think that this precaution is exaggerated or uncalled for, for between the author of a book and the reader there are relations established so intimate that they beget a kind of intellectual paternity, which produces deeper and more durable effects than you are aware of." The animus of the Church in reference to the discretion that ought to be exercised with regard to reading, we know from her legislation and the particular attention she has given to this matter. The severest penalties she decrees against those who read certain books. Even the sword of excommunication, which she herself directs with great and sober circumspection, she deems not too severe to unsheathe in this matter. Theologians may discuss whether and how far the law of the Index of prohibited books binds in different countries; one thing is obvious, that the great law of nature, imprinted by Almighty God on the tablets of the heart of each one, forbids us to read books that are the proximate occasion of sin. Not even the Sovereign Pontiff himself can give a dispensation to read such books. Do not follow Carlyle's advice of reading that which will give you most pleasure, for this is to pander to the inferior appetite. Read not for the sake of frittering away the time, for life is too short to be thus spent, and for each day, you can if you will, find a noble act to perform.

> "Clara, Clara Vere de Vere,
> If time be heavy on your hands,
> Are there no beggars at your gate,
> Nor any poor about your lands?
> Oh! teach the orphan boy to read,
> Or teach the orphan girl to sew;
> Pray Heaven for a human heart,
> And let the foolish yeoman go."

Read for the sake of instruction, and with instruction is always united intellectual pleasure.

www.ingramcontent.com/pod-product-compliance
Lightning Source LLC
Chambersburg PA
CBHW022112160426
43197CB00009B/991